Variation of Basic Motion	Comr ||D0969485
Adopt/Approve/Accept/Agree to	These ... main motion are interchangeable.
Add, or insert Delete, or strike out Substitute, or delete and add in lieu of	Any form that seeks to change the main motion is a motion to amend.
Postpone indefinitely Table	The motions "postpone indefinitely" and "table" should not be used.
Commit Recommit	The motion "commit" is restricted to referring a matter to a committee.
Move the previous question Move the question Call the question	All three variations using the word "question" mean to close debate and should not be used since they can be confusing.
	Allowed only when the question contains two or more independent matters.
Division (a standing vote or show of hands) Counted vote (roll call vote) Secret ballot, or written ballot Close nominations Close or reopen polls	A single member may demand a division. A roll call vote should require a 1/3 vote. All other motions should require a simple majority vote.
Rescind	A simple majority vote if the motion is made on the same day or the next day after the matter to be reconsidered was voted upon, or if notice of the motion has been given; otherwise a 2/3 vote is required.
Withdraw a motion Allow a nonmember to speak Dispense with the reading of the minutes (and approve them) Any request that does not require a suspension of the rules	The maker of a motion may withdraw the motion without a request if it is withdrawn prior to the Chair's stating the motion.
Limit or extend debate Amend the agenda after its adoption Take a matter out of its order on the agenda Adopt a special order of business Objection to consideration Any request that requires a suspension of the rules	Any motion that alters the usual right of members to speak requires a suspension of the rules. This motion can also include another motion, such as to suspend the rules and reconsider the adoption of the budget, in which case the motion to reconsider becomes undebatable.
	A tie vote or less than a majority vote causes the appeal to fail.
Recess	A recess is a brief adjournment. Although not usually amendable, if the motion contains a time to reconvene, it may be amended as to the time.

Praise for *Cannon's Concise Guide to Rules of Order*

"Hugh Cannon's book is great!"

— **Tip O'Neill,** former Speaker of the U.S. House of
Representatives

"Simple, understandable, and complete. All I think most people need
to know either to conduct a meeting successfully or to participate
effectively as a member."

— **Elizabeth Dole,** president of the American Red Cross and
former Cabinet secretary

"Hugh's book captures the common sense of parliamentary procedure.
It will help anyone, experienced or not, to understand a subject
that has seemingly become arbitrary and complex. In a friendly,
easy-to-read style, Hugh makes parliamentary procedure simple and
interesting."

— **Ron Brown,** Cabinet secretary and former chairman of the
Democratic National Committee

"A simple, understandable, precise, complete guide for the
chairperson of a meeting, most useful regardless of whether that
person is a novice or a professional. I recommend this book to all who
will be chairing a meeting, large or small."

— **Horace Mayo,** parliamentarian and former chairman of the
NEA Constitution, Bylaws, and Rules Committee

Cannon's Concise Guide to
RULES OF ORDER

Cannon's Concise Guide to

RULES

OF

ORDER

HUGH CANNON

*Parliamentarian of
the Democratic National Committee*

*Parliamentarian of
the National Education Association*

with Forewords by

Robert Strauss

*Former Chairman of the Democratic National Committee
and the Democratic National Convention, Former
United States Ambassador to Russia*

Mary Hatwood Futrell

Former President of the National Education Association

 HOUGHTON MIFFLIN COMPANY
Boston   New York

Library of Congress Cataloging-in-Publication Data

Cannon, Hugh.
    Cannon's concise guide to rules of order / Hugh Cannon : with
foreword by Robert Strauss, Mary Hatwood Futrell.
      p.   cm.
    Includes bibliographical references and index.
    ISBN 0-395-62130-5 (Hardcover)
    ISBN 0-395-73326-X (Paperback)
    1. Parliamentary practice.   I. Title.   II. Title: Concise guide
to rules of order.
JF515.C3213   1992
060.4'2—dc20   92-7385
                                                            CIP

To my wife Todd, for her
encouragement and support,
her skillful editing, and her generosity
of spirit.

CONTENTS

Foreword

Hugh Cannon was my parliamentarian over the years in the Democratic National Committee, at the National Democratic Charter Conference of 1974, and at the Democratic National Convention of 1976. I introduce him to you here, as I often did in person: "He is my parliamentarian and the best in America."

Hugh is not an academic parliamentarian. He is practical and pragmatic. He never wasted any time on the podium explaining why the Chair could not do something; he simply asked, "What do you want to happen?" and then he gave me an easy way to make that happen.

He has the experience because he has really been there.

He is my kind of parliamentarian.

This guide is straightforward, complete, and easy to use. It is also mercifully short. I get impatient with those who want to give me a lot more information than I need. I believe this book

will become a popular guide for all of us who want to run successful meetings, fairly and democratically, as well as efficiently. It
will definitely be a welcomed alternative for those who are put
off by the volume and the vernacular of other procedure books.

Robert Strauss

Chairman, Democratic National
Committee, 1972–1976
Chairman of the Democratic
National Charter
Conference, 1974
Chairman of the Democratic
National Convention, 1976
United States Ambassador to
Russia, 1991–1993

Foreword

Hugh Cannon served as my parliamentarian in my state association in Virginia and then later for the six years I presided over the national conventions of the National Education Association. Those NEA conventions were four solid days of serious issues, with over two hundred votes by approximately eight thousand delegates.

The difference that Hugh made for me was not the rules, although he followed those quite carefully. He somehow let me know that if I personally made contact with the delegates — communicated with them individually, even with eight thousand there — then the rules would become a lesser presence in the meetings. In fact, once I established myself with these delegates, and we trusted and respected one another, we never had to talk about rules at all. With confidence and trust established — what Hugh calls goodwill — all things became possible, and easily possible. It was like magic. It was like a romance of people. The issues, as you can imagine in a national two-million-member teacher advocacy association, were often sharply divided, and they were keenly and strongly fought — but there was always goodwill.

Our association has grown and continues to grow. I attribute some of this growth to the image and substance of our wonderfully successful national conventions. They are the most publicly visible demonstration of our purpose and unity.

This book, in which Hugh presents his system of successful presiding, as well as a clear discussion of basic procedure, fills the gap between the voluminous details of *Robert's* and the usually sparse standing rules of an organization.

It is user-friendly.

This book will be most valuable to presiding officers. But it will also be a basic primer for any member who wants to become more involved in the active workings of a meeting and of the organization.

Mary Hatwood Futrell
President, National Education
Association, 1984–1989

Why Another Book on Parliamentary Procedure?

*T*he fundamental message of this book is that the rules of parliamentary procedure are simple and should be used as little as possible. The presiding officer, whom I will call the Chair, can often dispense with the rules by winning the confidence of the members at a meeting and by building mutual goodwill. The Chair can then easily guide the organization's business to a timely and successful conclusion.

This can be done, it has been my experience, if the members and the Chair master the basic rules that are necessary for an orderly meeting. Once they are learned, the Chair can abbreviate procedures, expedite consideration of the items on the agenda, and generally facilitate action — and all with the consent of the members who understand what the Chair is doing and why.

The role of the Chair is to provide a fair, democratic forum for debate of the issues at a meeting and to ensure an accurate count of the votes of the members. It's that simple! Once the members realize that the Chair intends to fill that role, they support the Chair, allowing the person to move easily and freely in handling the business of the meeting. The members not only consent to be led by the Chair, they *want* the Chair to lead successfully. It's a little magic that happens in a meeting.

As a professional parliamentarian, I always have a thorough briefing before each meeting with the person authorized to preside, usually the president of the organization. This book contains all the essential observations, advice, and warnings that I review with the Chair in our briefings — a guide that has grown progressively shorter as I have honed it over the years, retaining the critical information and dropping the less important. I try to keep in mind — and impress upon the Chair — that parliamentary procedure is not some arcane exercise. *It is simply a common sense system designed to help groups of people make democratic decisions about matters of common interest.*

There is no single authority on the subject of parliamentary procedure and never has been, although *Robert's Rules of Order*, by Gen. Henry M. Robert, U.S. Army, published in 1876 and many times revised, is comprehensive and the best known in America. Thomas Jefferson's *Manual,* which he wrote for use when he presided over the senate as vice president of the United States (1797–1801) was the first well known book written in America; it is still used in the U.S. Congress. Rules of parliamentary procedure evolved over centuries and continue to change even now. Only those rules that traditionally have worked well continue to be used, although new rules occasionally prove to be helpful.

The presiding officer need not be intimidated by parliamentary procedure or any of the several ponderous books on its rules. All the Chair needs to know in order to conduct a successful meeting, in fact, is quite short and simple. But some academic writers have complicated what is actually not complicated at all.

England, the home of Parliament, the Mother Church of parliamentary procedure, has had available several short, well-written handbooks on parliamentary procedure for more than a century. America, on the other hand, has become more and more buried in successively lengthened and more detailed editions of *Robert's.* No one, of course, would question the substantial contribution of this famous writer. But his treatise, now published in a ninth revised edition, is more than seven hundred pages long and is filled with technical language that often confuses even skilled attorneys and parliamentarians. The average layperson is apt to be thoroughly bewildered by the thicket of rules and exceptions to rules, all couched in obscure language.

The English handbooks offer an instructive contrast. Sir Reginald Palgrave, a former Clerk of the House of Commons, wrote his concise *Chairman's Handbook* in 1877. The twenty-sixth edition, revised and published in 1964, is still written in understandable laypersons' language and is only a hundred pages long. Similarly, James W. Smith, an attorney in England, published his short *Handy Book on the Law and Practice of Public Meetings* in 1873. This eighty-nine-page handbook, revised through several editions over the years, remains a simply written, serviceable guide to basic parliamentary procedure. Yet another handbook widely used in England is Walter Citrine's *ABC of Chairmanship*, first published in 1939. This book of a little over a hundred pages states in its 1939 preface, "Whilst it is not claimed that the book deals with everything involved, it is an attempt to present the subject simply, adequately, and accurately."

That is the aim of this book. It sets out, for example, just twelve basic motions (as opposed to eighty-four in *Robert's*) that cover the matters most likely to come before meetings. These motions can be increased in number through extensive division, but the divisions are based on minor differences within a function and not on different functions. There are only twelve basic functions, and they are covered by the motions given here.

This book also declines to indulge in the many obscure terms employed in *Robert's* and by some academic writers. If a term can't be understood by an ordinary member at a meeting, it is not very useful. Therefore, this book is simple in its wording, spare in its motions, and focused on only the basic rules.

Yet a Chair who has won the goodwill of an assembly is not captive even to these basic procedural rules. It is the premise of this book that, if the Chair is successful in earning and receiving the goodwill of the assembly, the Chair acquires an ability to lead that goes well beyond that provided for by the customary rules. In many meetings, when the issues are complicated and extensive and time is limited, some decisions simply cannot be made unless the Chair has this ability. There may not be enough time for a large number of people to get through all their work using only the customary rules to arrive at democratic decisions. In these cases, it is essential that the Chair have the ability (given to it by the members during the meeting) to move ahead decisively — suspending rules if need be, limiting debate, cutting through a jungle of procedural detail — so that the members may democratically debate and decide all the issues before them.

I have worked as a professional parliamentarian for more than twenty-five years. Although my specialty is very large conventions — delegate assemblies of from 750 to 9,000 participants — I have also worked small meetings in many diverse situations. My purpose always is to help the organization have a successful meeting, whatever the size. To me, a "successful meeting" is one in which the entire agenda is considered, and considered on time; the members participate fairly and fully; the votes are accurately counted; and, most important, both the members and the Chair leave the meeting with satisfaction and pride in their organization.

This book has been designed to help any group achieve that kind of meeting. I first offer a brief overview that summarizes for those unfamiliar with formal meetings and parliamentary procedure the basic terms and concepts employed in this book. I then turn in Part I to explain in detail how a Chair — any Chair in any meeting regardless of size — can develop the goodwill so necessary for a successful meeting. The Chair who nurtures this kind of goodwill establishes a rapport with the assembly that makes reliance on rules as such much less imperative.

Then, in Part II, I focus on the members of the organization, the lifeblood of any meeting. Here I discuss how the members — through their role in the meeting and their work on committees — can most effectively participate in their group, contributing to its success and deriving personal satisfaction in return.

Because both the Chair and the members should have a good understanding of the ground rules of a meeting, I offer in Part III a short course in parliamentary procedure. The basic rules are laid out in language free from the technical jargon that has little relevance to ordinary speech. In addition, to quote Citrine, "I have avoided reference to authorities as much as possible as this is a tiresome process, but the reader may take it that the procedure laid down is quite authoritative."

The appendixes of this book offer model sets of standing rules and bylaws. These models in themselves can be instructive. In fact, to understand bare-bones parliamentary procedure, simply read carefully the model standing rules and you will have a reasonable grasp of the basic principles. The set of bylaws is essentially an outline that serves to describe the basic organization and functions of the typical association in the United States.

Finally I conclude with a glossary of terms used in the book, as well as a bibliography for readers wanting to pursue the subject further.

The book, then, has been organized to be used in a variety of ways. Read as a whole, it covers all aspects of organizational life and parliamentary procedure, but each of its parts is designed to address an individual need. Novices to the world of organizations and formal meetings; newly elected Chairs facing their first annual meeting; average members who would like to participate more fully in their group; organizations feeling the need to revise their basic governance documents — all will find specific, useful information here. And Part III, the heart of the book, is intended to serve on its own as a permanent, easily understandable guide to the rules of parliamentary procedure.

I have talked to some very capable presidents of organizations who have said that they have no problem with the management of their organization during the year, but they dread presiding over their annual convention. There is no need for such anxiety. My own experience with presiding officers who have expressed this sentiment has been that they can actually come to enjoy presiding, once they adopt the philosophy set out in the first part of this book. Chairs need never feel cornered or threatened — they have virtually unlimited resources, if only they are willing to develop them and learn how to use them to the best advantage. Members, too, by understanding what is going on and knowing they are participating effectively, will find the meetings they attend more enjoyable, satisfying experiences.

Acknowledgments

While I cannot name here the literally hundreds of presiding officers and thousands of members with whom I have worked over the years and from whom I have learned so much, still I would like to acknowledge several people who have been directly involved in the writing of this book.

First, I want to thank June Fisher, former president of the National Union of Teachers of England. June and I were introduced at a meeting a few years ago, and we fell to discussing the length and complexity of *Robert's Rules of Order.* June later sent me a copy of the parliamentary procedures guide used by her union and by the Labour Party in England: the 104-page *Citrine's ABC of Chairmanship.* This concise, thorough guide — well entrenched in the homeland of all parliamentary procedures — convinced me that a useful alternative to *Robert's* could find a place in American meetings. During my subsequent research, I received tremendous help from Mark Fisher, Member of Parliament, who took me on an illuminating visit to a session of the House of Commons, and from the staff of the Library of The British Museum, who were extremely kind and generous in making available to me their treasured books and excellent Reading Room.

My good friend, the writer John Stuart Cox, gave me much guidance and support in the early stages of writing and developing the book. Virginia Dalton, Ken Haller, and Horace Mayo, all professional parliamentarians, and Bernie Freitag, an experienced parliamentarian with the National Education Association, were unstinting in their skilled and constructive reviews of early drafts. For this paperback edition, I want to thank Gaut Ragsdale, a professor of parliamentary procedure and a professional parliamentarian, for his thorough review of the hardcover edition and for his helpful suggestions.

I appreciate, as well, the positive response to the book from various national organizations. The United States Information Agency has adopted it for U.S.I.A. sponsorship for translation and distribution in other countries. (Nepal was the first to request it.) The American Institute of Parliamentarians, an excellent national association of professional parliamentarians, reviewed this work and has included it on their list of approved books. The National Association of Parliamentarians carried a thorough and very favorable review in their publication *National Parliamentarian* and has placed the book on their list of works recommended to members.

Finally, I would like to thank Susan Boulanger, my editor at Houghton Mifflin, and Cecile Watters, the manuscript editor, for their help in bringing my ideas to the printed page.

Cannon's Concise Guide to
RULES OF ORDER

The Meeting: An Overview

A first formal meeting — one's introduction to parliamentary procedure — can be confusing and mystifying. The language is new, even strange. The process is very different from the way in which people ordinarily discuss matters and make decisions in their home or office. You may feel that you are in the middle of the process before you know even how to start. It's like being thrown into the deep end of the swimming pool before you know how to swim. But, as in swimming, the only way to learn is to venture in and try — with the help first of some basic instruction.

That is the aim of this overview: to provide to readers unfamiliar with parliamentary procedure the basic knowledge they need to follow and assimilate the information in this book. This summary will provide them with some understanding of most of the essential terms and the basic principles of the procedures of any meeting.

Readers already familiar with parliamentary procedure may skip this overview and proceed to Part I.

1

For those not familiar with parliamentary procedure, there are two inherent problems in reading a book on the subject. The first is the array of terms that are either foreign to the novice reader or have a wholly different meaning from their customary use. For example, *quorum* might be a new term to the novice reader, and the term *motion*, though a household word, has a very different meaning in parliamentary procedure. The second problem is the fact that unless the reader has a reasonable grasp of the whole parliamentary process from the outset, it is difficult to understand a discussion that necessarily deals with the different aspects of parliamentary procedure one at a time.

This overview is designed to address both problems. Terms in italics also appear in the glossary at the back of the book. I define each of these terms briefly here or give an example of its use, but the reader can also refer to the glossary for a more detailed explanation of the term.

I shall discuss how an organization governs itself and provides for the administration of its program. We will then see how the organization prepares for a meeting. At the meeting, the members deliberate over the matters that come before it and decide in a democratic fashion what position or action their organization will take on those matters. Then they end the meeting, maintaining a record of their actions, and the cycle begins again with preparation for the next meeting.

THE ORGANIZATION

The *organization* is a group of individuals with a common purpose who have voluntarily come together in an organized way. The organization has governance documents, usually *bylaws* and *standing rules*, which constitute a form of contract, or agreement, among these individuals as to the purpose of the organization, qualifications for membership, how the organization will be financed and governed, and how its meetings will be run. Sometimes an organization will also have a *constitution*, which serves the same purpose as the bylaws except that the constitution is more difficult to change than the bylaws. There are usually three levels of governance bodies: (1) the most powerful is an *assembly* of all the members; if there are too many members for all of them to meet together effectively, there may be a *delegate assembly* composed of delegates elected by smaller units representing geographic areas or organizational districts usually on some pro-rata basis (such as one delegate for each five hundred members); (2) a smaller group of members called a *board of directors,* usually elected by the members in their assembly, which governs the organization between meetings of the assembly; and (3) the *officers,* usually a president, vice president, secretary, and treasurer, and other officers as may be appropriate for the organization. Sometimes the officers are organized into a small committee called the Executive Committee, which may also include several other members. These other members are either specially elected to serve on the Executive Committee or serve *ex officio,* meaning that they automatically serve on the Executive Committee because they hold another key position (or office) in the organization; for example, the chair of the Budget and Finance Committee is often included *ex officio* as a member of the Executive Committee.

In addition to the three governance bodies (or individuals in the case of the officers), an organization may also have employed professional staff personnel. This staff varies according to the size of the organization and to its programs. The chief staff person is referred to in this book as an *executive director;* another popular title commonly used for this position is executive secretary. There is no established pattern to the titles of other staff members except that they usually reflect the function of the staff person — for example, the general counsel (the attorney) and the budget director.

Most organizations also have *committees,* which are appointed by the president or by the governance body of which they are a part. The assembly may have committees, made up of members of the assembly, and the board of directors may have its own committees, made up of board members. The bylaws stipulate how appointments to committees are made, the terms of their members, and their purpose or function. Committees provide for the administration of the organization's program and activities, such as formulating a proposed budget each year, reviewing and updating the governance documents and drafting proposed changes, and planning and supervising the election of officers. Committees work in all areas of the organization, doing all the detailed study and work (often with the assistance of professional staff) to develop policy statements, or *resolutions,* and implement projects in keeping with the purpose of the organization. The committee reports back to the members of the governance body to which it is responsible and presents recommendations for their deliberation and final decision; it may receive further instruction from the members as to an action the committee should take in the future. *Standing committees* function from year to year, fulfilling the continuing duties assigned them. *Special committees* are appointed for temporary duties and cease to exist once their special assignment has been completed.

MEETINGS

A meeting of the organization's members (or delegates) is usually initiated by *notice* to the members in the form of mailed information including the *agenda,* an outline of the items of business to be considered at the meeting with copies of the substance of those items; sometimes this information will be included in publications of the organization. The bylaws provide how often meetings will be held, sometimes the place (as in the headquarters building of the organization), and the details of the notice to be sent to the members.

A single coming together of the members is referred to as a *meeting;* a series of meetings is referred to as a *session.* For example, a convention might be a series of one meeting a day for four days; the four-day series is one session.

At the time and place announced in the notice, the president of the organization will normally *preside* over, or manage, the meeting. In the president's absence, the vice president, secretary, treasurer, or other officer will preside according to the order established in the bylaws. Regardless of which officer presides, that person is referred to as the chairperson or the *Chair.* The term *chairman* can be used when the Chair is male, but it should not be used when a female presides. I recommend the uniform term *Chair.*

The Chair presides over the meeting from the podium, usually on a raised platform, facing the members who are seated together on the *floor*. The Chair *calls the meeting to order* when the Chair has determined that the scheduled time has arrived and that a *quorum* is present, that is, the minimum number of members required by the bylaws to be present at a meeting in order for the assembly to do business. A quorum may also be established by a *call of the roll* in which the presence or absence of members is established by calling their names and receiving their responses, if present. In some larger assemblies, a *credentials committee* is assigned the duty of determining which members are present and legally entitled to attend and whether there is a sufficient number of members present to constitute a quorum.

The standing rules (often referred to as the *rules*) continue from meeting to meeting of the assembly and contain provisions for the conduct of the meeting, including how long a member may speak (such as five minutes), the order in which items will be considered, and the manner in which votes will be counted, or *tallied*. A standing rule can be *amended* by the members (that is, changed by additions, deletions, or a combination of both, called a *substitution*) at the beginning of a meeting, or a rule may be *suspended* during the meeting (that is, it will not be in effect during the time for which it is suspended).

The agenda is the list of items of business to be considered at the meeting. The list sent out in the notice is the *proposed agenda*. It is presented at the beginning of the meeting, and the members can amend it if they desire. Once the members have decided upon their agenda and adopted it, it is the *final agenda*.

MOTIONS AND DEBATE

A *motion* puts a matter or item of business before the assembly for its deliberation and decision, indicated by a vote on the motion. *Debate* is the process that takes place in the deliberative assembly after a motion is presented and before a vote is taken on it. Debate is made up of the discussions, or speeches, by individual members relating to the merits of the motion. Debate is sometimes referred to as consideration, as in the statement "The assembly considered the resolution for two hours before the final vote was taken." Thus, the three terms "debate," "deliberation," and "consideration" are interchangeable. Most of these speeches are for or against the motion because the motion is always presented in the form of a question to the assembly, which must be answered by voting either yes or no (with no middle alternatives). A speech, however, may also be neutral, such as an observation by a member that simply provides information about the subject matter of the motion. All speeches must be *germane,* which means that the speech must relate in some way to the motion being debated.

A motion can be proposed by a member or by a committee. Motions that have to do with substantive matters, such as whether to approve or adopt a budget, are called *substantive motions.* If the substantive matter is being proposed for the first time at that meeting, it is a *main motion,* though often referred to simply as "the motion." Other motions relate to the procedures in the meeting and are called *procedural motions.* An example of a procedural motion is the question to the assembly as to whether they wish to close debate.

A main motion is proposed, or *moved,* by a member and usually *seconded.* A second, which is customary but not necessary, assures the Chair and the assembly that there are at least two members in support of the motion.

Once moved and seconded, a main motion is then *stated* to the assembly by the Chair. This act of the Chair's *stating the question* is the Chair's determination, or *ruling,* that the motion is in order, which means that it is a proper and appropriate motion to be considered by the assembly at that time.

Debate begins with the opening statement or speech by the member who moved (proposed or made) the main motion. Once that member has spoken, the Chair then *recognizes* other members in debate in alternating order between those supporting the motion and those opposing it.

The main motion can be changed by a member's proposed *amendment,* which adds to it, deletes from it, or both. An amendment that both deletes and adds is often called a *substitute amendment,* or simply a substitute. The procedure for an amendment is similar to that for the main motion. The maker moves the amending motion, the seconder provides a second, the Chair states the question on the amendment, and then debate commences on the amendment.

The Chair, observing that no more members wish to speak, may close debate. The assembly may close debate by offering a procedural motion to *close debate,* which must be moved, seconded, stated but not debated, and voted upon.

All substantive motions, and thus all main motions, can be debated. Some procedural motions limiting or changing members' ability to speak in debate are not debatable. The most common nondebatable procedural motion is the motion to close debate.

VOTING

After debate is closed, the Chair *puts the question,* or proposes the question, to the assembly. The assembly makes its decision on the question by each member's voting, or answering yes (or aye) or no to the question. There is no alternative choice, other than the member's deciding to *abstain* by not voting at all. The Chair first attempts to determine which side has more votes simply by listening to the ayes and noes. If the Chair has any doubt about the result or if a member demands a visual vote, or *division,* the Chair first asks those who support the motion to stand and then those who oppose it to stand. In smaller groups, this division might be taken by a show of hands rather than by standing. The Chair then makes a visual determination of the division. If there is still doubt, the Chair or the members may decide to have a *counted vote,* in which each member is actually counted; a written paper *ballot,* in which each ballot is counted; or a *roll call vote,* in which each member's name is called out and the member answers yes (or aye) or no.

Most votes, and all substantive votes, require a *majority,* sometimes called a *simple majority,* for the approval or adoption of the motion. A majority is more than half. An exact split of the votes, half and half, is a *tie vote* and the motion fails for lack of a majority. The Chair does not vote except when that vote will make a difference, such as creating or breaking a tie vote. The one exception is a vote by written secret ballot, in which case the

Chair may cast a ballot along with the members. The Chair can vote only once, so if the Chair votes by ballot and there is a tie vote, the Chair cannot then vote to break the tie.

Procedural motions that limit or change the ability of members to speak in debate require a *two-thirds vote*. A two-thirds vote is sometimes also referred to as a two-thirds majority; this does not mean, however, that one vote over two-thirds is required. For example, if thirty members are voting, twenty votes fulfill a requirement for a two-thirds vote or a two-thirds majority. Governance documents, especially bylaws, usually require a two-thirds vote for their amendment. Standing rules may be amended by a simple majority, provided the members have notice in advance of the meeting; however, without notice, amendment or suspension of the rules requires a two-thirds vote.

Organizations sometimes use other majorities. For example, the vote required to amend the bylaws could be set at 60 percent, three-quarters, or any other percentage or fraction of the vote.

Some parliamentarians advise that the "simple" in *simple majority* is unnecessary and that *two-thirds majority* is redundant. These widely accepted and commonly used terms have become integral to contemporary procedure, however, and are used in this book to designate the specific vote intended.

ADJOURNMENT

Once the assembly has completed the agenda, the Chair can declare that the meeting is *adjourned*, or ended, and the assembly is over until the next meeting. The setting of the time for the next meeting is usually provided for in the governance documents, or it may be included in the motion to adjourn. The members may also decide to have a short adjournment, called a *recess*, and the assembly is not over but comes back together, or reconvenes, at the time designated in the motion to recess.

The substance of the matters considered at the meeting, and all decisions of the assembly, are memorialized in written *minutes*, usually prepared and maintained by the secretary of the organization and submitted for approval (or correction) at the next meeting of the assembly.

PART I
The Chair

CHAPTER 1

The Importance of Goodwill in a Meeting: The Effective Chair

I had been practicing as a professional parliamentarian for about ten years when I had a memorable and instructive encounter with Robert Strauss, the chairman of the Democratic National Committee and the initial presiding officer of the 1976 Democratic National Convention. I often relate this story when I am briefing a presiding officer with whom I have not previously worked because it demonstrates so clearly what I mean by the importance of the Chair's earning the goodwill of the assembly.

I was meeting with Bob Strauss well in advance of the 1974 Democratic National Charter Convention at which the party was to adopt, for the first time in its history, a charter that would be, in effect, a constitution setting out the party's basic principles. There would be intensive coverage by the national media. Chairman Strauss and I, with staff present, reviewed the basic procedures we planned to follow and discussed the problems that might arise. After this thorough meeting, Bob dismissed the staff and had a heart-to-heart talk with me.

He said, "All this is most important — these procedures, amendments, and details. I have confidence in you as a skillful parliamentarian to handle them. But now I want to ask you a more important question: 'Can you make me a hero in this conference?' "

You can imagine that at first his question startled me. But then, as we continued our discussion, I began to understand what he meant. His was, in fact, a critical and substantial question. It deserved an answer.

The national Democratic party was in a perilous condition in 1974. The 1968 convention in Chicago had been pure chaos, and the 1972 convention had been both hectic and tedious, with meetings lasting into the early morning hours. Bob Strauss had dedicated himself to bringing the party back to health and national prominence over the next two years. In presiding over a conference televised and reported nationally in the media, either he would come out a hero or the Democratic party would suffer. Strauss was experienced and skilled, and he knew that if this charter conference became mired in a procedural ditch, with irate, frustrated, or disgruntled delegates, there was little hope for the party's later success. On the other hand, if the delegates had a constructive, successful conference, in which a meaningful charter was adopted, and the Chair was judged to be an effective leader, then opportunities for future Democratic successes would be enhanced. Bob's wanting to be a "hero," far from being selfish, was prompted by his understanding of the importance of the Chair's role and of the absolute necessity for a successful charter convention.

I concluded our briefing session by giving Bob my commitment to work for a successful conference or, as he put it, to help him become a "hero."

The charter convention, in fact, went extremely well. As one journalist wrote in a magazine article reviewing the conference, there was "not only the perception of participation by all the delegates, but there was also the substance." Because of the broad spectrum of participants, there were many warring factions, and some issues were hard fought. But, in the end, all members were recognized and heard in a fair and open way; votes were taken, and taken accurately; and the members accepted the necessary compromises and the charter that was adopted.

Several weeks later, Strauss's picture appeared on the cover of *Time*. I took a black felt-tipped marker and wrote across the bottom, "You're a hero!" and mailed it to him. More to the point, the Democratic party returned to prominence within two years of that conference. Strauss, admired and respected as leader and chairman, had brought the many diverse groups together into a unified body that worked together successfully.

It is important to understand that in this context "hero" does not mean personal glory, but rather that the Chair has earned and received the goodwill of the members at a meeting. They become proud of their organization as they become confident in its leadership, and they bestow upon a Chair an authority that is more effective than that conferred by mere rules.

The meetings of an organization, especially its national meetings, provide an opportunity for building enthusiasm for the group. Present are its leaders, the people who will return home and report to the grass-roots members. It is essential that they report confidence and positive achievements rather than distrust and disruption. The local leaders are charged with recruiting members, collecting dues, and moving the organization's program forward. Satisfying, productive meetings build their enthusiasm and help determine their success or failure over the ensuing year.

The Chair makes the difference at meetings. If the Chair is an effective leader — focusing on the members, treating each fairly, earning everyone's trust — then the meeting will be successful. If not, it will end in disarray and fail to meet its objectives.

Effective chairing, or becoming a "hero" of the meeting, then, is not just frosting on the cake: a strong, purposeful Chair is essential. Nothing is as tedious or as distressing as a meeting that falls apart when a weak Chair loses the confidence and support of the members. This is disastrous for an organization.

CHAPTER 2

Earning the Goodwill
of the Assembly

*T*o become an effective Chair, the individual must establish goodwill, respect, and trust between the Chair and the assembly. The members, of course, have an important role to play, but the initiative lies with the Chair. That person should realize that trust won't come about automatically.

The psychology, or "feel," of a meeting depends on several intangibles: the Chair's sense of timing, the approach, and the general attitude the Chair conveys to the members. In this chapter, I will describe concrete ways — such as avoiding confusion and recognizing members fairly in debate — in which a Chair can translate these intangibles into a successful meeting.

The atmosphere of a meeting is much more important than the rules. If the atmosphere is bad, then not only will the rules not help, they will become a trap that ensnares both the Chair and the members. If the assembly becomes distrustful of the Chair, individual members may start to question the Chair's decisions, raise points of order about procedures, or otherwise inject themselves into a leadership role from the floor. When this happens, there is likely to be a clash of wills on every issue; the determination of the Chair and the resistance of the members escalate. If this happens, the meeting will undergo a precipitous downhill slide, both psychologically and practically, toward chaos.

Those serving as a Chair, then, must understand from the beginning that their role in a meeting is all-important and that they can establish an atmosphere of goodwill through the many small building blocks of initiatives taken from the opening to the closing gavel. There is no simple formula for building and holding goodwill, but patience and fairness will see most Chairs through the most difficult meetings.

WINNING CONFIDENCE FROM THE START: The Importance of Timing

Several aspects of the Chair's sense of timing are of major importance to successful gatherings. From the very beginning the Chair can show both control of the meeting and sensitivity to the members simply by starting the meeting exactly on time. The Chair should call the meeting to order at the hour noted in the schedule even if some members are still milling about in the halls or the meeting room. The Chair's choice is between respecting the rights of those who have arrived on time and the rights of those who have not. That choice should not be a difficult one. Reward those who, by being on time, have shown their commitment to the meeting.

A useful way to prepare members for this practice is to adjourn all meetings with a firm statement that the next one will start on time. Then, about five minutes before the meeting, the Chair can announce that it is about to begin and ask the members to take their seats. Though this would seem to be merely a matter of common sense, many Chairs fret over starting a meeting with even a few members not seated. But this only antagonizes the great majority who are in their seats impatient to begin.

Once the meeting has started, another aspect of timing comes into play. The Chair should be aware of how much is to be gained by proceeding slowly and patiently during the early stages of a meeting. When briefing a presiding officer before a meeting, I often draw a parallel between presiding over a meeting and courting. A deliberate approach at this point will go far to establish among the members a sense of the Chair's sincerity and fairness. Members need time to get the feel of the meeting, time to size up the Chair and decide whether the person can be trusted to make fair procedural decisions, take accurate vote counts, and deal with the members in a straightforward manner. Once their confidence is established, the members can sit back more comfortably — they have found their "groove" for the meeting — and the Chair, now in control, can proceed.

At this point, a little extra magic happens. In addition to building goodwill, the Chair has also created the impression among the members that he or she is a strong, competent person whom they are proud to have leading their organization.

The slow, deliberate approach during the early stages of the meeting applies also to the votes taken then. Early votes usually concern routine, uncontroversial matters, but they should not be rushed. The Chair should state all questions in a positive manner and restate them precisely before each vote.

The Chair should be especially sensitive and deliberate in ascertaining the results of each vote. When, for instance, a voice vote is taken that leaves any room *at all* for doubt, the Chair should, instead of announcing a result, ask for a *standing division* — that is, a vote taken by having those for and against a motion stand up. If, after the Chair has made a careful visual estimate of how many are standing for each side, the division is still close, the Chair, again without announcing a result, should call for a *counted vote* — that is, a vote whereby each member is counted individually. The Chair thus in these early stages systematically impresses on the members the high value placed on the accurate recording of their votes.

One practice I have found useful is for the Chair to ask for assistance at the podium in making the estimate on a standing division. This move takes a little more time, but it builds the members' confidence in the Chair. The Chair, for example, may ask for a second standing division, but this time requesting other elected officers on stage to assist in estimating the vote. (It is much better to use elected officers rather than paid staff for this assistance.) When the members stand, the Chair and the officers estimate the numbers in a very deliberate manner. After they confer, the Chair can announce that it is *their* opinion that the motion has passed or failed.

If the assembly has more than a thousand members, or if, because of the layout of the meeting hall, it is difficult to see all the members as they stand, there is another way to enhance the credibility of the estimate. The Chair can ask that members both stand and raise a sheet of white paper. The visual impact of the pieces of paper does make it easier to estimate the vote. But, more important, the members can see that the Chair has gone the second mile to call the standing vote accurately.

Of course, if the standing vote is still too close to call, then the Chair *must* take the time to conduct a counted vote. This is especially important during these early stages. Counted votes are time-consuming, but they impress upon members the Chair's determination to be fair and accurate. Having built this kind of trust, the Chair will find in later stages of the meeting that the members tend to allow the Chair to call for standing divisions rather than counted votes every time. The assembly has come to have confidence in the Chair's estimates.

What the Chair is conveying to the members by these actions is this message: "You took your valuable time to come to this meeting. In return, I shall take time with the matters that concern you. What's important for you is important for me. I will be attentive so that you will be heard; you will know exactly what you are voting on; and the vote count will be accurate. I will not rush you or misrepresent your intentions."

Successful Chairs should also keep in mind a third aspect of time. Some meetings have extensive agendas that will be difficult or impossible to complete within the meeting's allotted time if the normal procedures and time limits of debate are observed. There are simply too many items to be considered and too many people to be heard.

The National Education Association (NEA), for example, holds annual assemblies of eight thousand delegates during which more than two hundred items of substantive business are considered and voted on — in four days. On the last day, the lack of time within which to complete their work often forces the delegates to limit debate severely. Each member's speaking time is reduced, usually to one minute, and often the number of speakers per question may be limited to two for and two against. Other restrictions on normal parliamentary procedure may also be imposed.

It is at a moment like this that the Chair reaps the benefits of the time spent in the first days establishing goodwill and confidence among the members. If they trust the Chair and are aware that time is running out for completion of their business, they will be willing to suspend the rules and adopt a custom-tailored procedure so they can finish on schedule.

Another example of this sort of situation was a meeting that was held a few years ago by the California State Employees Association, which was considering a new constitution and bylaws. Given that these are basic governance documents, the many issues were critical and detailed. Time was running out on the last day, but the Chair had carefully built goodwill in the earlier days through a generous expenditure of time on each delegate. The Chair, observing now that time was short, proposed on her own initiative that all rules be suspended and that the assembly adopt a new set. These rules called for alternating speakers (limited to two minutes) for and against each issue, permitting no amendments or other motions, and requiring a straight up-and-down vote by the assembly on both documents at a specific time. See "Special Orders," pages 76–77, for a description of this procedure. This proposal was adopted unanimously. Without goodwill, the members would have hooted at such a drastic move. Instead, they trusted the Chair and saw that the proposed procedure was a realistic solution to their problem of time. The Chair had earned an authority that superseded the ordinary rules.

These two examples, though not typical, dramatize my point that the wise use of time can be an asset. Expended early in the meeting, time can build the goodwill necessary to meet any exigencies that might arise later.

MAINTAINING FOCUS

Concentrating on Each Individual

A Chair looking out over any assembly of more than fifty members is apt to see them as a single group rather than as individuals. This perception, however, can be overcome. When an individual member is speaking, the Chair should focus on that person and remain attentive until the member sits down or moves away from the microphone.

In one rather common situation, the Chair recognizes a member and then, realizing that the person is not really speaking to the point or is perhaps expressing an eccentric point of view, disengages and lets the member continue without focusing attention on what the person is saying. The consequences of such a lack of focus can be very damaging. The member may rattle on and then suddenly make a motion, such as a floor amendment. The Chair will be caught off guard, with no idea what the motion is or whether it is in order. Forced to acknowledge this inattention, the Chair must request that the member restate the motion. At that point, the member who was speaking is, in effect, more in charge of the meeting than the Chair, who does not know what is going on. When this happens, there is apt to be a buzz about the assembly hall because it is clear that the Chair has lost control, if only for a few moments. Although the damage may seem negligible — the motion can be restated and everything put back on track in a short time — the assembly's confidence in the Chair has been shaken and will not be easily regained.

A similar error can occur if the Chair loses focus and disengages attention from a speaker who then asks a direct question. The Chair must admit inattention and ask that the question be repeated. The members will grow uneasy, and the familiar buzz will sound through the room. Everyone realizes the Chair wasn't paying attention to the business at hand and, moreover, apparently didn't value this member's role in the meeting. Some others may infer from this that the Chair doesn't value their role either. The Chair here has not only failed to build goodwill, but has lowered the assembly's estimate of the Chair's fairness and effectiveness.

The Chair must avoid this kind of error. It costs too much in lost confidence and it can easily be avoided if the Chair pays careful attention to each individual and remains focused on what is going on at all times.

When briefing a presiding officer before a meeting, I always stress that every member present has invested time, and usually money, in order to attend the meeting. Even if the Chair does not think that a particualr member's viewpoint is important, the reality is that members of the assembly respect the role of each member and feel that each has a right to be heard, to be taken seriously, to make motions and to ask questions. If the Chair denies a member these rights through inattention, the assembly will doubt the Chair's fairness and diligence.

All members — no matter how discourteous their manner or irrelevant their positions — must be dealt with seriously and with grace.

Avoiding Procedural Distractions

Members of an assembly always know if the Chair is focused on or distracted from the meeting. Even in large meetings, with several thousand members in attendance, there are tell-tale signs that I have noted above that indicate when the Chair is not focused. But in practice, it is often difficult for the Chair to maintain concentration in the face of a meeting's many distractions. There are, however, some specific ways to defend against them.

The biggest offender is apt to be the staff. These individuals are usually very keyed up by the meeting. They are preoccupied with the many "housekeeping" details involved in a large meeting. They will frequently come up to the podium during the meeting to consult with the president — asking questions, running errands, and transmitting messages from members. Sometimes they simply want to demonstrate to the president how hard they are working "even during this dull meeting." They can, however, become a huge distraction to the Chair.

To avoid this problem, the Chair must make the podium off-limits to staff. Only one key person, such as the executive secretary, should be available on the podium, and only that person should be allowed to talk to the Chair while the meeting is in progress. The Chair usually needs some staff assistance so that any housekeeping question asked by members can be readily answered; but staff members other than the key assistant should be under strict orders to stay away.

Other members, especially past presidents who obviously only wish to be helpful, may also distract the Chair during the meeting. This problem is more difficult to handle than that of the staff because staff can be given firm instructions beforehand. Members, on the other hand, cannot, and they will attempt to give advice, carry messages, or just come up to chat. There are times when a member wants to show the back-home delegation that she or he has access to the podium and the ear of the Chair.

Security guards at either side of the podium are the best answer if that is politically expedient. Volunteer members (who can be warm and friendly) are just as effective as commercial security if they are carefully instructed. If it is not possible politically to post security guards, the next best approach is for the Chair to make a clear, straightforward announcement at the outset of the meeting that, because the business of the meeting is so important and time is so short, members are requested not to approach the podium while the meeting is in session. The Chair should point out that it is not possible to preside effectively and carry on conversations at the same time; the Chair may then graciously offer to meet with members during recesses and at the end of the meeting.

Avoiding Substantive Distractions

A Chair's focus may also be blurred by matters of substance. When briefing a presiding officer before a meeting, I am often told that there will be only one or two major issues and that the other items will pretty much take care of themselves. This comment never fails to alarm me because in my experience the opposite is often the case. When a presiding officer voices this attitude, I quote this verse from the Old Testament:

> Catch us the foxes,
>   the little foxes
> that spoil the vineyards.
> (Song of Solomon, 2:15)

The grower may have built a sturdy wall about his vineyard to keep out the large marauders, but he is reminded to be concerned about the *little foxes* — they can slip through the smallest holes in the wall and spoil the grapes.

Certainly, the big issues can dominate a meeting: they entail

longer, more emotional debates, with more members seeking recognition and making motions. But precisely because so much
attention is given to these issues, the Chair can usually keep
them well in hand. It's often the small issues that have not been
anticipated and prepared for that can develop into serious distractions, interfering with the smooth running of a meeting. Mind
the little foxes — always.

ENSURING BASIC FAIRNESS

The Importance of the Chair's Impartiality

Basic to the parliamentary system is the impartiality of the
Chair. If that person and the members become adversaries, then
the Chair's decisions — from recognition of members to procedural rulings — can become highly suspect. The Chair may be
perceived to lack basic fairness. (There is no need to define "basic
fairness" here. The courts, when adjudicating legal questions
that turn on the issue of due process, have often concluded that
due process is simply a matter of "basic fairness," assuming that
most people readily agree on what that is in a given situation.)

A Chair cannot enter into a debate in any way without com-
promising the impartiality of the office. Thus, if possible, the
Chair should not be lured into answering questions by members
if to do so would appear to align the Chair with one side or the
other of an issue before the assembly. This can be a troublesome
matter if the Chair believes that the questioner seeks information
that is relevant and significant to the debate, but realizes that the
answer may enhance one side of the argument. In that case,
the Chair must respond in an appropriate fashion, according to
personal judgment. The Chair, after all, is usually the president,
the person in the organization most likely to be able to provide
basic organizational information.

If the Chair is strongly concerned about an issue and feels
compelled to enter a debate, the Chair should relinquish the podium and speak from the floor. It is better then for whoever takes
over the role of Chair to continue presiding over the meeting

until the issue under debate is put to a vote. Then the Chair can return.

Preventing Confusion

The perception among members that a meeting is being conducted with basic fairness requires that there be no confusion, no sense among the participants that they don't understand what is happening. Confusion can easily lead to distrust, especially among large groups of people, and confusion and distrust can easily build out of proportion to actual events. The result is that members feel they have not been treated fairly. They may even leave the meeting convinced that the confusion was deliberately staged so they would not know what was "really going on." It may seem to some that a "hidden agenda," unknown to the rank and file, was maneuvered through a smoke screen of confusion.

The easiest tool for avoiding confusion is repetition. Before any vote on a substantive motion, the Chair should restate the motion in such a way that there can be absolutely no misunderstanding as to what is being voted upon.

- If the motion has been written down and all members have copies, the Chair should refer to it and specifically identify the proposed motion by page and item number.

- If the Chair has the only written copy, then the entire motion should be read. If it is lengthy, that is the maker's problem, not the Chair's.

- If the Chair does not have a written copy, then the meeting should be stopped until a copy has been provided. Or a Chair who does not want to stop the meeting should call on the maker and direct that person to restate the motion. If the person makes obvious changes in the original motion when restating it, the Chair has no choice but to insist that the motion be put in writing. Never call a vote on a "floating" motion — a motion that the maker has changed during debate. In this situation, ask that the item be deferred until the motion can be written down and read by the Chair.

Another area of confusion concerns a motion to close debate; this is often stated as "moving the previous question" or simply the "question." If the Chair uses either of these terms, the assembly can easily become confused as to what it is voting on.

For example, a member says, "I call for the question." There is a second. The Chair turns to the assembly and says, "The question has been called. All in favor, say aye. Opposed, no."

Did everyone really understand what was meant? Were the members supposed to be voting on the main motion, what they thought of as the "question" before them? No, the assembly was voting on the "previous question," which means only to close debate. (This antiquated form originated in the British Parliament, but it is no longer used even there.)

Two practices will forestall confusion of this sort. First, the motion to close debate, regardless of the term a member uses in making the motion, should always be stated by the Chair in those words: the "motion to close debate." And, second, when the vote being called for is on the main motion itself, the Chair should always clearly restate the motion. Avoid short cuts such as "Well, I'm sure we all understand the motion, so let's just take the vote." In short, the Chair must be absolutely certain that everyone understands what's being voted on.

A chilling effect can come if, ten minutes or so later, a member rises and announces, "I didn't understand what we were voting on back there, and I think this meeting is being railroaded." The Chair should always be able to say flatly, "I'm sorry you didn't understand the motion. Let me remind everyone, however, that I carefully read the text of the motion in its entirety. I could not make it clearer than that, and I believe that most everyone else understood what we were voting on. I'm sorry you did not."

A Chair who can't make that statement is in trouble, and as painful as it may be, the best solution is to take a second vote on the motion in question.

Admitting Mistakes

The Chair's procedural mistakes can also be injurious to the members' perception that a meeting is being conducted with basic fairness. We are, however, all human and mistakes happen. When a Chair realizes a mistake has been made, what can be done about it?

The answer is simple: acknowledge the mistake immediately and correct it. Never attempt to bluff. Bluffing usually does not work, and moreover, it is insulting to the assembly for the Chair to assume that the members can be hoodwinked. Admitting a mistake does not make the Chair less effective or authoritative; on the contrary, the Chair can benefit from this demonstration of honesty.

The most dramatic example in my experience of an admission of error occurred during a four-day convention of eight thousand members of the NEA. At the end of the third day's meeting several members came up to the podium and reported that they had sent forward an amendment that should have been recognized and considered before debate had been closed and the main motion adopted as the last item of business that day. Since all this had happened very quickly at the end of the meeting, they had not had an opportunity before adjournment to raise a point of order — that is, an inquiry of the Chair as to why their request to make an amendment had not been recognized. When we examined the documents at the podium, we discovered that these members were in fact correct. Their request had been overlooked in the closing moments of the day's meeting.

The next morning, as the first item to come before the assembly, the Chair explained our oversight. This Chair had earned great respect for her patience and fairness, and she said now, in effect, "We made a mistake up here at the podium. This proposed amendment from the floor should have been recognized. Without objection, we will go back to that point in the debate on the main motion [as though it had not been adopted the day before] where these members should have been recognized for their amendment."

Usually, an assembly's going back in this fashion would require a motion for reconsideration, a second to the motion, debate on the motion to reconsider, and a formal vote. But in this case, the Chair simply stated that "without objection" the assembly would go back without using any of those parliamentary procedures. There was no objection. (See "Decisions by Unanimous Consent," pp. 124–125.)

Notable here is the fact that among eight thousand members, there was no objection. Everyone appreciated the Chair's honesty and straightforwardness in acknowledging the error (which was clerical, in fact, and clearly not her fault), and they readily agreed to its correction. This was an example of chairing at its best.

If goodwill has been established at a meeting, corrections can usually be made without dissent, and the perception of the Chair's basic fairness will be enhanced.

Effective Communication Between the Chair and the Members and Recognizing Members Impartially

The Chair, in fulfilling the role of impartiality, should use an even hand in recognizing members to speak. When there are two sides to an issue, recognition should alternate between those members for and those against it.

Several years ago, the California State Employees Association (CSEA) asked me to advise them on the procedures of their biennial conventions. Their conventions had so many disruptions that the assembly could not complete the business on their agenda. Members were angry, and the Chair was constantly attacked for the way meetings were being handled. I asked that they send me a copy of the verbatim transcript of their last session. My reading of the transcript revealed a basic problem in their procedure. With about nine hundred delegates present, they had not adopted a system for the fair and effective recognition of members who wished to speak. Each had to shout out for recognition at a dead microphone. Only when the member was recognized was the microphone activated and the member able to speak through the microphone-speaker system. The CSEA had used nine microphones, and often many more than nine delegates were clamoring for recognition at the same time. The result was chaos. Much meeting time was consumed in arguments about a delegate's not being recognized or complaints that the microphones were monopolized by members on one side of an issue.

The answer was simple. We put in place a card recognition

system whereby members who wished to be recognized would go to a numbered microphone and take one of four colored cards there. They would hold it up so that spotters at the head table could see them. Green was a sign of wishing to speak for the motion on the floor; red was a sign of opposition; white was a sign for wanting to ask a question; and blue indicated a point of order. To make a main motion, to propose a floor amendment, or to close debate, either the red or the green sign could be used.

The spotters at the head table had corresponding smaller cards with the numbers of the microphones on them. The spotter would first hold up the corresponding card so the member at the microphone would know that the request for recognition had been received. Then that card was placed on the table next to the podium in correct order for the Chair. Green and red cards were placed in alternating order, for and against, so both sides of the issue would be heard. Blue and white cards were moved ahead of green and red cards, since they indicated matters to be recognized before the others. The Chair then simply picked up the cards, with absolute impartiality, in the order in which they were arranged by the spotters. The effect of this system on the CSEA's next convention was dramatic, and a major part of their problem was eliminated.

The card recognition system is simple and inexpensive. It eliminates shouting for recognition, and it provides for much more balanced and fair debate.

Recognition systems using telephones, such as that developed by the NEA for its conventions, are even more effective but require more expense for equipment and larger numbers of people to operate. Each numbered microphone has a telephone and a telephone monitor. The member approaches the monitor, who accepts the member's recognition request and then telephones the podium. Clerks at the podium receive the requests for recognition and prepare slips of paper bearing the member's name, microphone number, and the purpose for which the member seeks recognition. (A telefax system could also be used to transmit this information from the floor to the podium.) These slips are then passed along the front tables to the Chair. Meetings large enough to require such systems usually deal with complex issues, and it is wise to have a professional parliamentarian arrange the slips in proper order before passing them to the Chair.

In 1976 a modified version of the NEA telephone-recognition system was put into place at the Democratic National Convention to eliminate the constant shouting for recognition that had disrupted the 1968 and 1972 conventions. The reduction in confusion and noise was dramatic. (Additional factors contributing to the change were the primary system of nominating presidential candidates, which has meant that the nominees are, in effect, already chosen before convention time, and current convention rules that afford almost no opportunity for recognition of individual delegates on the floor.)

Whatever the system, the Chair should ensure the fair recognition of members with a minimum of noise and confusion.

The recognition of members is under the control of the Chair, but when the members understand that they will be recognized fairly, their sense of participation and of free communication with the Chair is greatly enhanced. The psychological goodwill of this more effective communication between the members and the Chair ensures a more successful meeting.

MAKING GOOD USE OF YOUR PROCEDURAL TOOLS

Occasionally delegates at an assembly will approach me as the parliamentarian and ask how they can get control of the meeting through the use of procedural rules. I always answer, "It's easy. Become president of the organization!" The Chair has every opportunity to use procedure to assist in the control of meetings.

The Chair — usually the president — has influence over all the events that take place *before* the meeting, and it is those events, more than any other factor, that determine the course of a meeting. The most skilled and likable leader cannot be a good presiding officer without careful, detailed, and painstaking preparations.

I often counsel larger organizations to prepare a complete verbatim script for their presiding officer. I have written many of these myself, and there is no substitute for laying out every move, every word, for a meeting. This is probably not necessary for small monthly meetings of a few members, but an important meeting should always have a verbatim script prepared for its presiding officer. Only in this way can the Chair foresee every motion and the openings for floor amendments and other member-driven actions that can interfere with the Chair's achieving the goals of a meeting.

The script makes clear what procedural tools are available to the Chair and when they should be used.

The Agenda: The Chair's Mandatory Map

The agenda, as the map that an assembly agrees to follow throughout the meeting, is a powerful tool.

One of the primary roles of the Chair is to anticipate all the business that is necessary or appropriate to come before the meeting and to make suitable preparations. For that reason, the Chair usually has the opportunity to prepare the proposed agenda, which is mailed out to the members prior to the meeting. Even in those cases in which the organization assigns this duty to a committee, the Chair (the president) is always the key member of that committee. In all cases, the Chair has more influence than any other member in the preparation of the proposed agenda. That is an advantage that should never be neglected.

The adoption of the final agenda for the meeting is a decision of the assembly itself. The proposed agenda is open for debate and amendment, but the Chair has a strong psychological advantage in having it printed and distributed. The members' amendments are offered from the floor and are usually not printed or distributed ahead of time. Floor amendments are always at a disadvantage for that reason.

Also, because the adoption of the agenda comes in the very early stages of the meeting, the members, as I pointed out earlier, are usually unsettled and not focused yet on serious business. In fact, the adoption of the agenda is, in practice, often handled as a pro forma ritual in much the same manner as the adoption of the minutes (the written record of the previous meeting, usually also printed and distributed). If the members don't pay close attention, the Chair's map of the meeting becomes locked in, and the assembly must follow that agenda until adjournment.

As will be discussed in more detail later, the only substantial matters that can come before the assembly are those main motions (and, for those, there must be a formal motion) provided for on the agenda. Floor amendments are an exception in a sense, but even they must relate to (adhere to) the substantive main motions on the agenda. Once the agenda is adopted, the meeting is basically settled as to content, and surprises as to substance will probably not occur.

The assembly itself is permitted to change the agenda later, but in practice it is quite difficult to do so. Passage of such a later amendment requires a two-thirds vote because, it is reasoned, it should take an unusual vote to change what members have come to expect and are prepared for. There are other disadvantages in trying to change the agenda. Members almost never have copies of proposed changes; they are not distributed. Also, they may wonder, if the matter was so important, why they weren't given written notice, or at least the courtesy of some notice, at the time the agenda was adopted at the beginning of the meeting.

The Chair can capitalize on these disadvantages by gracefully, and reasonably, observing, in effect, "I know you consider this new item of business you want added to the agenda to be very important. It may well be. I think, however, that everyone realizes that we are now at the end of the meeting, and we all agreed when we adopted the agenda that this is all that we would consider at this meeting. You did not propose this item then, so we had no notice of it." In this way, the Chair can make certain that members are fully aware of the unusual nature of a last-minute effort to change the agenda.

To be sure, the Chair is also locked into the agenda, but, remember, the Chair had the opportunity to prepare, or had the most impact on, the agenda, and should, therefore, have less reason to want to change it during the meeting. A Chair who nevertheless wishes to do so and who has followed the recommendations of this book and earned the goodwill of the assembly, will be in a much stronger position to suggest a possible change than will most members. This move has its dangers, however; as soon as the members agree to go along with the Chair's desire to change the agenda, they see no reason they, too, shouldn't change it. It's safer not to open the door to changes in the first place.

The Disciplinary Nature of a Motion

The Chair should exercise strict discipline and control over the meeting by not allowing members to speak unless there is a motion on the floor. No motion, no talk — it's that simple. (See, however, Chapter 11, "Initiatives from the Floor.")

The Chair needs to keep this fact clearly in mind. A motion can be requested by the Chair ("May I now have a motion that the minutes be approved as distributed?"); moved by a committee ("Motion that the credentials report be adopted"); or moved by a member ("I move that this item be postponed until the next meeting"). But there should be no discussion of anything until there *is* a motion on the floor, and all members know exactly the question to be decided and can focus on making that decision.

Governing by the Rules

There is no way that the Chair can approach a meeting without confidence concerning the basic rules of parliamentary procedure — the short course laid out in Part III of this book. If the Chair has a professional parliamentarian who participates in the meeting continuously, then, of course, the Chair can rely on that person to some extent. Nevertheless, the Chair should also have a firm grasp of the basic principles of parliamentary procedure.

In large meetings — those with five hundred or more participants — the Chair will be greatly helped by employing a professional parliamentarian. This individual can monitor the system used in the meeting to recognize members and can keep an accurate log of all the business as it progresses. The parliamentarian focuses on procedural details — the motions, the amendments, the recognition system — which frees the Chair to focus on individual members and what each is saying. This is a near-perfect division of labor, splitting the responsibilities of the Chair between two people who can pay close attention to their particular domain at all times, thus enabling the Chair to do a much better job of presiding.

The Card System

To coordinate the efforts of parliamentarian and Chair, I sometimes use a card system I worked out about twenty years ago. At the time, I was the parliamentarian for a constitutional convention of about five hundred delegates of a very large national organization. They had spent weeks together hammering out their proposed constitution. Several months later they were scheduled to spend three days making final decisions on the document. But then the Chair was in an automobile accident. The vice-chair had to take over on short notice, and he and I met an entire day to plan for the first meeting.

There was a serious problem. The vice-chair was hearing-impaired and feared that he would not be able to hear both the delegates (who would use a microphone to speak) and me, his parliamentarian. We solved the problem by developing a card system, in which I placed a three-by-five-inch index card on the podium for each motion so that the Chair could visually follow the progress of the meeting by referring to the cards. The emergency situation had forced me to develop a system that has now become a most useful tool for my work as a parliamentarian.

The system requires a professional parliamentarian who is solely responsible for preparing the cards and making the system work. Since it is visual, the system eliminates the need for most verbal communications between the parliamentarian and the Chair. The Chair is never distracted and can focus almost entirely on listening to the members.

The writing on the card is necessarily a brief, or shorthand, description of a motion, not its full text. For example, a three-page resolution might have a card that reads "Resolution No. 26, The Environment." An amendment might simply identify the maker: "Charles Morgan's amendment." The card is a prompt only, not a substitute for the text of the motion which the Chair should have separately on the podium.

Procedural motions, such as the motion to close debate, are

set out on cards previously prepared by the parliamentarian. They are more helpful to the Chair if they include a script, or the parliamentary wording, that the Chair is to use when the procedural motion is put to a vote. A notation, placed at the bottom right-hand side of the card, is a reminder to the Chair of what is required for the motion to pass and whether or not it is debatable. That short notation reduces the Chair's memory work substantially. See pages 35–39 for illustrations of cards prepared for the twelve basic motions of parliamentary procedure. On the back of each card, the parliamentarian may include notes from the parliamentary authority prescribed by the organization.

The cards are held in place by small clips attached in a line along the side of the podium with sufficient intervals between cards so that each card is completely visible to the Chair at all times. The cards are placed on the side of the podium for practical reasons: they are out of the way, and where the Chair will not inadvertently move them or cover them with texts of motions or other papers, and the parliamentarian can handle them without reaching across or disturbing the Chair. The Chair can follow these prompt cards at all times without losing focus on the audience or on the written texts in the middle of the podium.

Most podiums slant down from the top, which lies in the direction of the audience, toward the bottom, in the direction of the person at the podium. Thus, the order in which the cards are placed — from top to bottom — is the logical sequence and is also the standard parliamentary sequence. With no business before the assembly, there is no card. When business starts, a main motion is made and a main motion card is placed at the top position. If an amendment is proposed, the card for the amendment is placed in the second clip just below the main motion card. A motion to refer both the main motion and the amendment to a committee would be placed in a third, lower clip, and so on.

The Chair always deals with the bottom card because it represents the last motion made, the last card placed in line, and thus is the pending motion. By "pending," I mean the motion that is presently before the assembly and that must be considered and acted upon before any other motion. Once the pending motion

```
Main Motion

Chair: The question is:
       Shall we adopt_____
       _____
       (the main motion)?

Chair: All in favor of adoption, please say
       aye.
       All opposed, please say no.

Chair: The main motion is (not) adopted.

                           Simple Majority
                           Debatable
```

```
Amend

Chair:  The question is:
        Shall we amend by adopting_____
        _____
        (the specified amendment [to be read
        in full whenever feasible])?

Chair:  All in favor of this amendment,
        please say aye.
        All opposed, please say no.

Chair:  The amendment is (not) adopted.

                            Simple Majority
                            Debatable
```

Sample cards for coordinating meetings (see page 33)

Postpone

Chair: The question is:
         Shall we postpone this matter until
         _____(time to which postponed)?

Chair: All in favor of postponement, please
         say aye.
         All opposed, please say no.

Chair: This matter is (not) postponed.

                              Simple Majority
                              Debatable

Refer

Chair: The question is:
         Shall we refer this item to the_____
         (committee, board)?

Chair: All in favor of referral, please say
         aye.
         All opposed, please say no.

Chair: This matter is (not) referred.

                              Simple Majority
                              Debatable

Close Debate

Chair: The question is:
         Shall we close debate?

Chair: All in favor of closing debate,
         please say aye.
         All opposed, please say no.

Chair: Debate is (not) closed.

                              2/3 Vote
                              Not Debatable

Divide the Question

Chair: The question is:
         Shall we divide this question_____

         _____
         (in the specified manner)?

Chair: All in favor of dividing this
         question in this manner, please say
         aye.
         All opposed, please say no.

Chair: The question is (not) divided.

                            Simple Majority
                            Debatable

Roll Call Vote

Chair: The question is:
         Shall we take a roll call vote on
         this matter?

Chair: All who want a roll call vote, please
         say aye.
         All opposed, please say no.

Chair: We shall (not) take a roll call vote.

                            1/3 Vote *
                            Not Debatable

Reconsider

Chair: The question is:
         Shall we reconsider this item:_____

         _____?

Chair: All in favor of reconsideration,
         please say aye.
         All opposed, please say no.

Chair: This item shall (not) be
         reconsidered.

                            Simple Majority
                            Debatable

*I recommend a one-third vote requirement; the rules of an
organization may specify a different vote.

```
Request to the Assembly

Chair:  The question is:
        Shall we grant the request_____
        _____(specify) made by_____
        _____(member's name)?

Chair:  All in favor of granting this
        request, please say aye.
        All opposed, please say no.

Chair:  The request is (not) granted.

                              Simple Majority
                              Not Debatable
```

```
Suspend the Rules

Chair:  The question is:
        Shall we suspend the rules to_____
        _____
        (accomplish or prevent a specified
        result)?

Chair:  All who want to suspend the rules,
        please say aye.
        All opposed, please say no.

Chair:  The rules are (not) suspended.

                              2/3 Vote
                              Not Debatable
```

```
Limit Debate

Chair:  The question is:
        Shall we limit debate to_____
        (number) speakers for and_____
        (number) speakers against, with a
        limit of_____(number) minutes per
        speaker, and limit points of
        information to_____(number)?

Chair:  All in favor of limiting debate,
        please say aye.
        All opposed, please say no.

Chair:  Debate is (not) limited.

                              2/3 Vote
                              Not Debatable
```

Appeal

Chair: The question is:
          Shall the ruling of the Chair be
          sustained?

Chair: All who favor sustaining the Chair,
          please say aye.
          All opposed, please say no.

Chair: The Chair is (not) sustained.

                              Simple Majority
                              Debatable

Adjourn

Chair: The question is:
          Shall we adjourn?

Chair: All in favor of adjournment, please
          say aye.
          All opposed, please say no.

Chair: We are (not) adjourned.

                              Simple Majority
                              Not Debatable

Recess

Chair: The quesion is:
          Shall we recess_____(for a specified
          period of time or until a specified
          time)?

Chair: All in favor of a recess, please say
          aye.
          All opposed, please say no.

Chair: We are (not) in recess.

                              Simple Majority
                              Debatable

is handled, that bottom card is removed, and the next card up the line becomes the pending motion. For example, let's say a main motion and a motion to amend have been made. The motion to amend card would be clipped below the main motion card. The Chair would then know that the pending motion is the amendment. Once the amendment is voted on, that card is removed, and the main motion card remains to tell the Chair that the pending motion is now the main motion (as amended or not).

Once, in a large convention, a vice president was asked to stand in for the president for a short while. With no time for further preparation, I told him just to read the cards. About forty-five minutes later, the president returned and the vice president said to me as he left the podium, "I wondered how our president was doing this so well. Any member, if he could read, could run this meeting with those cards."

His comment was obviously an overstatement. But the card system does relieve the Chair of any anxiety over what precisely is before the assembly and should be acted upon next. The Chair is in full control of the meeting at all times.

I remember another occasion when seven hundred delegates were gathered at a meeting of the Wisconsin Education Association Council. They were engaged in a stormy debate over a difficult issue, and there were eight motions pending at the same time. On a point of order, a member at the back of the hall complained that there were so many motions "no one in this room has the slightest idea where we are and what we are debating!"

Their president, sitting comfortably atop a high stool behind the podium, answered quickly, "Oh, yes. I know exactly where we are." He then read off the eight cards in the proper order. He received a standing ovation. Everyone settled down, and the delegates successfully worked through all the pending motions. This Chair was a "hero" — he had earned the confidence and goodwill of that assembly.

Handling an Appeal of the Chair's Ruling

One of the more useful tools for a Chair is the appeal. As will be seen in Part III (p. 115), an appeal is a motion by which a member challenges a ruling stated by the Chair. A vote of the assembly is taken, and the members decide if they will support the Chair or the challenging member.

On its face, an appeal would appear to be a negative item for the Chair, but handled carefully, it can become a powerful asset. The critical factors are timing and substance.

For instance, an appeal at the very outset of a meeting puts the Chair in a difficult position. Most members, as I've said, are still unsettled. They haven't yet fully focused on the meeting nor found the comfortable groove that comes a little later. Once they have, members are much more supportive of the Chair, but until then, they are easily disturbed. Fortunately, if the agenda has been properly planned, there is usually no occasion for controversy early in the meeting. The first items on the agenda tend to be matters of formality, such as rules and the minutes.

But what if someone does appeal? In that case, the Chair should let the member explain the reason for the appeal and then ask for a moment to confer with the parliamentarian, other officers, or whoever is appropriate. If the challenge clearly has no basis and is frivolous, the Chair — after this conference (which tells the members that the Chair is serious, fair, and deliberate in making any judgment) — can then rule, explaining the reasoning behind the ruling and reminding the assembly that others on the stage have been consulted. A totally frivolous appeal will surely fail if it is handled this carefully. On the other hand, if the member is clearly correct, the only solution is for the Chair to announce that, after careful consultation, the appealed ruling will be modified to agree with the member's challenge.

There is another alternative in the early stages, which is an option the Chair has at any time during the meeting when it is clear that the member's challenge has merit and there is a question of substance at issue. In that case, the Chair can put the question to the assembly. This approach saves face for both the Chair and the appealing member: the assembly becomes a neutral judge in a matter that has two solid, though conflicting, points of view. The Chair states that there are two sides to the issue, briefly restates both sides, and then (without a motion) puts the question to the assembly. There is seldom any negative fallout, psychologically, no matter which way the vote goes.

Using Appeals to Gain Support for the Chair

So far, we have talked about how to handle an appeal in the ordinary way. Now let's look at it as an opportunity for the Chair to strengthen the Chair's position or sometimes simply to get a quick reading of a potential vote.

Assume, for example, that the meeting has progressed into more controversial matters on the agenda. The formal items — credentials, rules, agenda, reports of officers — have been completed and the members have settled into the meeting. Now a very controversial issue comes under debate and a member becomes antagonistic toward the Chair concerning some small matter about how the debate is proceeding. The member may not have an actual appeal in mind, but the person can't let go of what is essentially a trivial objection. The exchange between Chair and member becomes prolonged, and the assembly grows restless.

At this point, the Chair stops and says, "I understand what you are saying and your position, but I am also ruling you out of order because we need to proceed with the debate on this most important matter. [Without pause] Do you wish to appeal this ruling by the Chair?"

The member, usually taken aback at this turn of events, asks, "What do you mean?"

The Chair replies, "I am ruling you out of order and you must take your seat. Now, you may appeal this ruling if you like. All you need to do is say, 'I appeal.' Do you appeal?"

Invariably, the member says, "I appeal."

Although the motion to appeal is, in fact, debatable, it is more nearly procedural in form, and the Chair can usually put the question immediately without debate by simply saying, "All those who support the Chair, please say aye. Those opposed, say no." Notice that the focus of this wording is support of the Chair, not the procedure. (Remember that we are talking about a situation in which, first, because we are well into the meeting, we will not violate our rule of avoiding risks during the early part of the meeting, and, second, real substance is not involved — that is, the member's issue does not have real merit.)

In this situation, the vote to support the ruling of the Chair will usually be overwhelming, with the only negative vote coming from the challenging member. I have heard eight thousand "yes" votes in support of the Chair and only one "no" vote at NEA conventions.

The psychological effect of such an overwhelming voice vote is amazing. Even though the members of the assembly do not feel strongly one way or the other (remember, there is no real substance at stake), they will be impressed by the enormous support for the Chair, whose image usually rises correspondingly.

This tool must be used with extreme care, however. The Chair is actually trying to gain the members' psychological support by forcing the member into an appeal. This should never be attempted during the early stages of a meeting or when there is real merit on the side of the challenging member. The tactic, obviously, is more effective in larger meetings of five hundred or more people. In a smaller meeting, though the vote would be proportionately the same, it would not have the same psychological impact.

The Chair may also use this tactic to take a quick straw vote to test the strength of a particular group in the meeting. If the opportunity arises, the Chair forces an appeal by a member who is clearly a leader or representative of that group. The vote on the appeal will give the Chair a reasonably good idea of how many votes the group will have on the main motion. Again, however, the Chair should not risk this tactic unless the timing is favorable and there is no real substance to the question.

Using Unanimous Consent to Gain Support for the Chair

As will be seen in more detail in Part III (pp. 124–125), unanimous consent is a most useful motion for moving ahead quickly when the matter is not controversial and there is no objection.

This procedure is used by the Chair, not the members. The Chair usually states the desired result (such as correcting the wording of a motion) and then states, "Without objection, that correction will be made in this motion. [*short pause*] There being no objection, the motion is corrected."

The principal purpose of this procedure is to save time —

forgoing the usual forms of motion, debate, and vote when it is clear that all agree — but its use can also build confidence in the Chair.

For example, a main motion has been made and debate is underway. It soon becomes apparent that there is a problem with the main motion as it is written. Unfortunately, the first amendment proposed to correct the problem misses the mark and would in fact only complicate matters further.

At this point, the Chair simply says that the consensus seems to be that the members wish to make a small correction in the main motion. The Chair then says, "Without objection, we will make that correction in the main motion and the amendment will be withdrawn. Is there objection?" Assuming that the Chair has assessed the situation correctly, the correction is made and the amendment withdrawn — all without further motion, debate, or vote.

This little move is relatively simple. The members of the assembly, however, do not necessarily see it as simple. They tend to be very pleased that their Chair, the leader they elected, can cut through parliamentary procedure and set matters right. The Chair is focused on the issue and is in control of the business before the assembly. Again, the Chair has gained a little more goodwill, and the members are confident that the meeting is going well.

Handling Points of Personal Privilege

Points of personal privilege (discussed in detail on pp. 116–118) arise when a member seeks recognition to speak to a matter not on the agenda and not before the assembly. The point the member wants to make has some relevance to the organization but not necessarily to anything before the assembly at that time. There are two types of points of personal privilege. The first category concerns situations in which there is some obstruction to a member's ability to participate effectively in the meeting. The microphone in the member's area of the hall is not working, for example, or the sound system is not reaching that part of the hall. This first category of points of personal privilege requires immediate attention and poses no threat to the orderly conduct of the meeting.

The second category of points of personal privilege, however, is quite different. Say a member was supported by the organization in a recent labor dispute and now calls for a point of personal privilege in order to thank the organization publicly. The point demonstrates generosity of spirit and is well intentioned. A similar example would be a point made to introduce to the assembly a member who has recently received some recognition that brings credit to the whole organization. Again, the purpose is noble, but with a large assembly, a number of such points can continue for a considerable time.

Though often harmless and even interesting to some degree, these points of personal privilege always pose a major risk to the success of a meeting. The danger here is that once the Chair has opened the door for points of personal privilege, other members may see the opening and rush through. A very time-restricted meeting can suddenly bog down with a dozen or more points of personal privilege, each taking several minutes or more. An hour or so can be lost at a meeting in which every minute is needed for crucial business. A carefully planned agenda has been taken over by individual members.

This can be a no-win situation for the Chair. The Chair is viewed as weak if an individual is allowed to hold 99 percent of the assembly hostage to matters that, though related to the organization, are certainly not vital to the meeting at that moment. On the other hand, by arbitrarily silencing members who, in good faith, believe they have some item the assembly should hear about, the Chair will appear harsh. (One might question, if this particular point was so important, why wasn't the item put on the agenda by the member in the form of a resolution? In fact, the item is seldom that important.) My solution to this problem is to head it off from the beginning — before the first point is even attempted by a member.

This solution is set out in Standing Rule 20 in Appendix A, which I recommend that organizations adopt. In it, I divide points of personal privilege into the two categories described above. The first, which I call "*procedural* points of personal privilege," relates to those situations in which the members' ability to participate effectively in the meeting is threatened, such as the sound system failing in part of the hall. The Chair is obligated to recognize a member making this kind of point of personal privilege immediately and to propose some remedy to the problem. Points in this category require emergency attention but do not consume much time.

The second category includes every other point of personal privilege, and it is this category that poses problems for the Chair. These points are designated as *"nonprocedural* points of personal privilege." In the rules, the Chair is given discretion about when to recognize these points, but, since the individual should not be totally at the mercy of the Chair's discretion, the rule also provides that these latter points should be recognized immediately prior to adjournment.

If the assembly adopts this rule, then it is the members of the assembly, not the Chair, who have made the tough decision about points that are not procedural. The individual member won't be as happy, but responsibility for the decision has been shared.

If the Chair can't get Standing Rule 20 adopted, then the next best choice is to announce during the early stages of the meeting (before members attempt to make points of personal privilege) that though the Chair intends to recognize points of personal privilege, they will not be allowed to interrupt the business that the members have adopted as their agenda. Those who wish to be recognized for a point of personal privilege should send up a note giving the Chair their name and a short description of the point. Then the Chair can hold off recognizing these members until just before a recess (as for lunch) or at the end of the meeting. Lacking a rule, the Chair can outline to the assembly a practice that resembles the rule. Because this procedure is usually accepted as reasonable by the members, the Chair thus diffuses any emotion that might result when members already have the floor but are then induced to stop talking and defer the point until later. This situation has a chilling effect on members, no matter how gently the Chair makes the request. It may even be better at that point to let the member continue. By doing so, however, the Chair may be opening the door for others to seek recognition for their points.

PART II
The Members

Because the Chair is the most visible person in a meeting and has the most potentially dramatic role, we often focus too much on that person and not enough on the individual members. But without the members, of course, there would be no meeting; nor will the meeting be effective if the members are not. This part discusses ways in which members can become more effective participants.

The democratic goal of a meeting is centered on full and open participation by all the members. All too often the institutional management of an organization (whether that management is the elected president and other officers, or an employed professional staff leader, such as an executive secretary, or a clique of members, or some combination of these) establishes the "smooth" meeting as their primary goal. Unfortunately, to management "smooth" too often means a meeting that moves through the agenda quickly with little or no discussion, much less any real debate, and that results in strong (preferably unanimous) approval of all the proposals put forward by management. In effect, sometimes management wants a simple pageant, not a democratic meeting. These conflicting goals — full and open participation by the members and a smooth meeting — are almost always irreconcilable. Obviously, the members who wish to participate effectively will side with the goal of participation. Fortunately, an enlightened management will have the same goal.

Part II discusses the options and opportunities of the individual member who seeks to participate — that member's goals, duties, rights, and tools (the ways or approaches) for reaching the goal of full and open participation.

I want to emphasize again that the whole thrust of this book is that the most effective and successful organizations have meetings that are truly democratic. Conflict between management and members is not inevitable: it can be easily avoided. Open, vigorous debate of issues of substance on the floor of a meeting is part of the democratic goal, not conflict in the negative sense.

I shall discuss the most effective ways in which a member can prepare for a meeting, well before it is held, in order to become familiar with the substantive matters on the agenda and the rules to be followed in the meeting. Next, I identify some positive steps a member can take at the time of the meeting in order to participate more fully. Finally, I focus on committees, the most useful means by which a new or inexperienced member can enter the mainstream of participation in the life of the organization.

CHAPTER 3

The Members' Role

So often I have seen well-meaning members become frustrated in a meeting as a result of not being able to take part in the meeting effectively. They may be intelligent, but they are simply unfamiliar with the detailed, complex question being debated. On the other hand, they may understand the issue, but not the rules of debate, and they make mistakes with motions and timing — all to the great annoyance of other members. The other extreme are members who don't do anything. Whether out of timidity, a lack of preparation, or passiveness, these members simply sit and watch while others make the decisions and manage the organization.

The goals of every member in a meeting should be to understand the issues, to debate freely those issues when debate is appropriate, to express their views clearly, and to make certain that their votes are counted correctly.

Though their achieving these goals depends partly on the Chair, the organization's bylaws and rules, and the expectations of other members (e.g., are they accustomed to no debate? do they accept a dictatorial Chair?), individual members still have control over a number of ways in which they can participate effectively.

Members should remember that they have both rights and duties in meetings — the right to enter into debate and to have their votes correctly counted and the duty to do everything necessary in order to be ready to participate. I hope that I conveyed in Part I the importance of the effective Chair's preparing extensively and thoroughly before the meeting starts. This lesson applies equally to the member. Careful preparation is essential for both.

PREPARATION BEFORE THE MEETING

As a first step in preparation before going to the meeting, the member should become familiar with the governance documents of the organization — the bylaws and standing rules. (See Chapter 5, "Governance Documents.") These documents don't have to be memorized, but the member should obtain copies to read and then take them along to the next meeting of the assembly. No one can absorb in one or two readings all that will be contained in fully detailed governance documents, but the member can consult these documents at the meeting, especially the standing rules, to follow the way in which the agenda is handled, debate is conducted, and votes are taken. The documents and the practice should follow essentially the same pattern. The member will better understand the documents by seeing them put into practice.

The next important area of preparation before the meeting is a careful review of the agenda and research and study of the items on the agenda so that the member will have a reasonable understanding of what is to take place. This book strongly recommends that the agenda and copies of all substantive matters to come before the meeting be mailed to the members in ample time for their careful review as well as any necessary study. (See Chapter 6, "Agenda.") This notice before the meeting gives the member the opportunity to become almost as well prepared for the meeting as the Chair. Generally speaking, a member will not be equally interested in every item on the agenda and will give close attention to only those matters of personal interest. In any event, the individual should not neglect this excellent opportunity to prepare for those matters that are personally important.

Later in this chapter, I will discuss how the individual member can add items of business to the agenda.

ARRIVAL AT THE MEETING

A seemingly small consideration, but in fact a most important one, is for the member to arrive well in advance of the meeting. Depending upon the custom of the organization, a member often can come about thirty minutes early and visit with other early arrivals. Invariably, if there are any critical issues scheduled for the meeting or any news concerning the organization, the halls outside the meeting room will be abuzz with discussion.

It is also a general practice for the leaders of a particular position on an issue that is to be debated and voted on at a meeting to come early to test the waters with the early arrivals. The alert member who also arrives early thus has a chance to hear discussion about the issues, as well as the usual rumors about which side will prevail, who is supporting what, and other political details of the organization. Rumors shouldn't be taken too seriously, but they do provide a notion of what's to come up at a meeting and sometimes they can be accurate.

Another reason for members to arrive early is so they can select a place to sit. This can be of some importance. If a member intends to speak, then a seat reasonably close to a microphone or the podium is a good idea. Some thought on how the Chair recognizes members will affect the decision on where to sit.

If there is any question about being recognized at the appropriate time, the member would do well to approach the Chair before the meeting begins and ask for recognition on the appropriate question. The Chair will usually agree to this request at this time, but it is also wise to hand the Chair a three-by-five-inch card or a half sheet of paper, which bears the member's name, where the member is sitting (e.g., "at microphone number 5" or "in the center of the front row"), and the item on which the member wants to speak (e.g., "Resolution No. 9").

If the Chair is using a parliamentarian who has some impact on the order of recognition, then giving a similar note to that person is also helpful. I recommend contacting both, since even if the parliamentarian hands the note with the name to the Chair at the appropriate time, the Chair might have several members seeking recognition at once, and it will be preferable for the member to have some earlier commitment from the Chair.

Members sometimes feel that approaching the Chair to ask to speak may seem presumptuous, especially if the member does not know the Chair personally. But that is not the case. Individual members should always be encouraged to contact the Chair, for the Chair needs to know who the willing speakers are. Even if there is no opposition on an issue, the Chair will still want several speakers so that the assembly will have a good sense of the support for the issue rather than experience the negative feeling that can result if an item is adopted with little or no debate.

PLACING AN ITEM ON THE AGENDA

Now that we have discussed the ways in which a member can become prepared for the meeting and the steps to take at the meeting in order to participate, we take up the more difficult matter of how the member might bring a substantive matter before the meeting as an individual, not as part of management or as the representative of a committee. In other words, how can members initiate matters of special interest to themselves?

The surest way to have an item brought before the assembly is to have it added to the agenda. There are two opportunities for an individual member to do this. The first, if the recommendation of this book is followed, is to include the item in the proposed agenda that is mailed out to members with the notice for the meeting. (See Standing Rule 4, Appendix A.) This will require the member to prepare the motion (or floor amendment; see pp. 103–105) early, wording the item carefully, so that it will be clearly understood and appropriately drafted for its intended purpose. If the member wants to change the dues, which are set in the bylaws, then the appropriate motion must be in the form of a proposed bylaw amendment and meet the notice requirements for such an amendment. If the member wants to propose a resolution, then the form of the motion should follow the format customarily used by that organization.

The second opportunity for a member to add an item to the agenda is when the proposed agenda is placed before the assembly for its adoption as the final agenda. At that point, the proposed agenda can be amended, and the member has an opportunity to propose an amendment from the floor adding the item to the agenda. The process of amendment from the floor has several drawbacks, however. First, the member has to be alert to be recognized by the Chair. The adoption of the agenda is usually considered to be a mere formality, and the Chair can easily overlook a member trying to make a floor amendment. The second drawback is the requirement that a majority of the assembly must agree to add the item, and before they will agree, the item will be debated. Generally speaking, assemblies are reluctant to add items to the agenda unless there is a compelling reason. They feel that they received notice with the proposed agenda in the mail and that other items shouldn't be brought up at the last minute. In my experience an assembly's attitude toward floor amendments to the agenda is almost always negative.

Because of these drawbacks, it is much better for an individual member to send in any proposed item of business in time for it to be included on the originally prepared agenda. There are several advantages to this approach. For one thing, the member is assured that the item will be considered. Another factor is the psychological importance of having the item printed and mailed to the members. The item gains stature and substance because of its appearance in print with prior notice. An amendment from the floor is never perceived by the members to be as important as the printed one they hold in their hand. The floor amendment seems to be merely a last-minute thought. The psychological disadvantage can be substantial.

If the member fails to have a proposed item added to the agenda, there is still another course that can be taken and that is by way of a floor amendment to something already on the agenda. This approach, however, shares all the drawbacks to floor amendments discussed above and entails a further problem. Is there an item on the agenda that can be appropriately amended with the individual's proposal? Remember, the floor amendment must reasonably relate to the main motion it seeks to amend; it must be germane. If there is no relevant item already on the agenda, there is no opportunity for the member's floor amendment to be considered. A sympathetic Chair might allow some latitude, but the assembly will seldom tolerate a totally irrelevant floor amendment.

Sometimes a proposal from an individual member is *necessarily* a floor amendment — for example, an amendment to a committee report the member knows will be presented at the next meeting. In this case, the member should plan ahead for the floor amendment. Since, as we have seen, a printed item has more status than a verbal one, it would help the member's chances to file a copy of the proposed floor amendment and ask that it be included in the notice to all members. Once again, the member is psychologically in a stronger position if the proposal, even a floor amendment, has been printed and mailed to the members.

Assume, however, that the member fails to meet the time deadline and the proposal cannot be mailed out with the agenda. The member should then have enough written copies of the proposal prepared before the meeting so that they can be distributed to each member before the amendment is proposed from the floor. The means of distribution varies with the size of the meeting; copies can be placed in the members' seats prior to the meeting, or they can be handed out at the appropriate time. At large meetings, such as the NEA Representative Assembly, the staff often goes to great lengths to help the individual member achieve full distribution of a proposed floor amendment. The NEA will reproduce the full text on a large overhead screen, provided that the staff receives the text in sufficient time for its preparation for the screen.

PARTICIPATING IN THE MEETING

I have devoted the greater part of this chapter to the member's preparation for the meeting because that early groundwork is so important. But I have some additional suggestions that should be helpful to the member during the meeting itself.

A small but potentially important matter concerns seconds. If the organization, by rule or custom, requires a second, the member should have someone ready to second the motion immediately after it has been moved. If there is a prolonged pause while the Chair waits for a second, the delay may cause some members to wonder if there is any support for the motion. The surest approach is to move the item and then, for example, add, "And John Smith, at microphone nine, will second this motion." With this announcement, there is no pause and no question of support.

Another area of concern is the matter of challenges to the Chair. One of the worst mistakes a member can make is to challenge the Chair simply because a rule is not being followed with technical precision, that is, when the error does not in fact affect the substance or the fairness of the business at hand. This mistake is most often made by a member who is well schooled in parliamentary procedure and wishes to demonstrate this skill to the assembly. A challenge of this sort is especially annoying when a very good Chair is picking up speed and cutting a few corners on procedure — and with the support of sympathetic members who realize the meeting is being run fairly. Even if the challenging member is technically correct, the Chair may force an appeal and the assembly more often than not will support the Chair, regardless of the infraction. (See "Points of Order" and "Appeals," pp. 114–115.)

What purpose is served by a challenge? If the member has no other objective than to attempt to demonstrate to the others some technical knowledge of procedure, then no purpose is served. Instead, the "correct" member is apt to gain only hostility from the others while the Chair earns much goodwill. Certainly, if the Chair deprives a member of substantial rights, a challenge is in order. But a meeting is not a classroom for parliamentary procedure to be taught to the assembly by one member. In my experience, most members don't particularly like procedural rules anyway, and the procedural challenges are often just an irritant.

As a last observation, I want to emphasize that the surest route to effective participation in the meeting itself is to be well prepared to debate the substantial issues. In debate, there is no substitute for in-depth, comprehensive knowledge of both the overall concept and the details of a subject. Even poor speakers can hold the attention of an assembly if their comments are informative and interesting. On the other hand, a good speaker with nothing to say soon becomes a bore.

To be both a good and an informed speaker takes time, study, and practice. I encourage members who are attending their first meeting to start right in, as long as they have a contribution to make. But they can maximize that contribution by thoroughly studying their subject beforehand and honing their skills as a speaker. For that, nothing takes the place of practice.

CHAPTER 4

Committees: A Route to Participation

A newcomer's most effective means of entry into participation in an organization is by way of a committee. Composed of fewer members, it is more informal and thus less structured and less demanding as to rules and procedures than the full assembly. It is not so intimidating and thus is more accommodating to the new or inexperienced member who wishes to participate in the organization.

Membership on a committee not only offers newcomers a way into an organization's inner structure, it provides the means for those who are not officers or appointed leaders to influence the organization's direction. While committee members may not be as visible or play as dramatic a role as do assembly leaders, they can be influential behind the scenes in gathering and presenting information and in forming and promulgating policy.

Remember that organizations rely heavily on committee

reports as the basis for assembly decisions concerning finances, policy, governance, and future direction. Individual committee members who focus diligently on their committees' duties and procedures and on the personalities and goals of their fellow committee members can nudge the committee — and thus its proposals for the assembly — in directions compatible with their own goals for the organization. In this way, committee members affect the life and future of the organization.

The committee system is widely used by most organizations. It is also highly recommended in this book for several reasons. The primary purpose of a committee is to provide a means by which a particular matter may be carefully considered by a small group of members and then be brought back to the larger assembly for a decision. The assembly, in effect, delegates the detailed, often time-consuming research and study to a more informal group that can take whatever time is needed to consider the matter. The group then develops a plan or proposal for the assembly to debate and adopt, either in the same form as the proposal came from the committee or as amended by the assembly. The assembly can also reject a committee's proposal or send it back for further consideration.

TYPES OF COMMITTEES

Standing committees are those established in the governance documents of the organization. They continue in existence, or "stand," from year to year, considering the matters assigned to them and making proposals on a continual basis. The budget and finance committee, for example, is always a standing committee because the financial matters of an organization continue ("stand") throughout its existence.

Special committees function in the same way but are created for a special assignment. Depending upon the governance documents, special committees may be created by the president, the board of directors, the assembly, or some combination of these. The assignment may continue for months or even years, and thus the special committee could take on the appearance of a standing committee; but its usual assignment is a single project, and once the committee reports back to the assembly, its mission is over and it ceases to exist.

BECOMING A COMMITTEE MEMBER

Committee participation offers to new members an opportunity to become involved in the business of the organization. Or a member of many years who has been relatively inactive may move over into the participation stream through a committee. The member will find a more receptive and comfortable environment as compared to the more formal procedures of the meeting of the assembly itself.

Of course, becoming a committee member can sometimes require some effort on the part of the individual. Membership on committees varies with each organization and its political pressures. But my experience over the years has led me to conclude that the individual who really wants to work can find a congenial assignment.

The first step for the individual is to read the governance documents of the organization in order to learn which committees are standing and which are special; how each is appointed; how many members each has; when terms begin and end; and, especially important, how vacancies are filled. A record of both standing and special committees is usually maintained by the secretary or the business office of the organization.

The next step is to obtain a list of the standing and special committees of the organization, the names of the committee members, and the details of their terms (when each member's term began and when that term is to end). Generally speaking, terms of standing committees will be staggered, which means that part of the membership changes each year. A typical example would be a committee of six members, all of whom serve three-year terms with two expiring each year. This overlap of membership assures continuity within the committee: there will be no more than two new members in a given year, with four experienced members continuing their terms. Special committees could have staggered terms in the same way as standing committees, but because these committees usually have a limited time assignment, the terms may all be the same or may all end upon completion of the assignment.

Often a review of the committee lists will disclose that there are vacancies. Someone resigned or died or a term expired and a new appointment was not made. Sometimes, in the case of an organization whose president appoints members to committees, the president will hold in reserve a few vacancies, waiting until there is some especially useful purpose to be served in filling them. This purpose can sometimes be purely political. Appointment to a committee is a time-honored means for a president to reward members for providing political support — and also a practical way for the president to exercise control over the organization by placing friends and supporters on the committees that provide the direction and leadership for the group. More often, however, these vacancies are simply a matter of the president's having run out of members who are interested in the work of the committee. Not wanting to load the committee with deadwood — members who don't care and won't work — the president leaves the vacancies open for the time being.

Whatever the reason for them, these vacancies represent opportunities for an interested member to approach the president and request an appointment. When the vacancy exists for political reasons, the president will weigh the appointment carefully. But usually the president will just be waiting to find someone genuinely interested in working.

If the board of directors makes the appointments, the individual should still follow the process I have just described. In this case the president, who is almost always the presiding officer for the board of directors, will have to take the matter to the board for approval. Even if the board alone has authority to appoint, the president will still be the person who initiates the process. The only exception to this is the rare case in which the board has its own nominating committee; even then, the president is usually the most influential member and thus the key person to contact. In short, when there are vacancies, go to the president and ask for help in becoming a member of a committee.

What if the vacancy is on a committee whose work assignment is totally foreign to the member? So what? The only way for an individual to get started is, in fact, to get started. Consider, for example, an English teacher who wants to become an active participant in the work of a school organization, but finds that the only opening available is on the budget and finance committee. The teacher may feel that finances are anathema, but he or she should jump in anyway. Remember, at this stage the goal is to find an entry point for participation, not to demonstrate knowledge and expertise. These will come in time.

To continue the example, one of two things will happen. In the first instance, the teacher will attend the meetings of the budget and finance committee and become substantially better informed about an otherwise unknown area of the life of the organization. Although not fascinated with the subject, perhaps even mystified by it, this member will inevitably learn more about it and, more to the point, learn how the committee system works. And opportunities may still arise for positions on other committees. Should a vacancy occur on the program committee, this member can approach the president and say, "I have attended every meeting of the budget and finance committee. I have learned a lot about how this committee system works, but I believe I would make a more valuable contribution if you switched me over to the program committee." This teacher, then, is way ahead of the member who might have declined the president's appointment to a certain committee because of lack of interest.

The second possible result in our example is that the teacher, to the amazement of all, including herself, becomes an expert in budget and finance matters. There is a need for a mix in committees. In this example, the committee might have been composed of six of the most knowledgeable and experienced CPAs in the organization, but perhaps none of them could write and present a clear narrative report to the assembly. It's possible that the English teacher, assuming some capacity for comprehending numbers, could develop into the role of spokesperson and chair of the committee. Leadership must be developed, even in those born with an ability to lead.

The member who seeks to participate but finds that there are no vacancies should nevertheless follow the same process. First, a vacancy might occur at any time and, second, by researching the process and making personal contacts, the member is in a better position when appointments are to be made.

COMMITTEE OPERATIONS

The committee itself operates through procedures that parallel those used in the meeting of the assembly, but the committee is much more informal and operates with fewer restrictions in debate. (See Chapter 7, "Committees.") Therefore, the new or relatively inexperienced member will be much more comfortable and can participate at the committee level from the very first meeting.

Because the committee is composed of so few members — relative to the number of members in the assembly to which the committee reports — even those procedures that apply to the committee can often be dispensed with in favor of informal discussion and consensus. It should be remembered that the committee members have usually been selected because of their knowledge and experience in the subject area and their willingness to do the work assigned to that committee. In this atmosphere, the committee chair can often simply start the meeting by stating the specific objective of their work at that time and then allow members to speak at will without the process of recognition and no limit on the number of times a member can speak. This informal discussion can often lead to apparent agreement among the members, and at that point the chair announces that there seems to be consensus on the matter, and the committee's report will reflect the consensus. If there is no objection, there need be no motion or vote. The committee members have simply agreed among themselves.

The committee, then, is the most accessible means of entry for the individual member seeking to participate actively in an organization. It is a place where much information and insight concerning the group can be gained and also a place where parliamentary skills can be developed at a comfortable pace. Through committee participation, both the newcomer and the non-office-holding member can quietly but substantially affect the operations of the organization, its future direction, and its policies on issues vital to the organization and its members.

PART III

The Meeting: A Short Course in Parliamentary Procedure

Introduction

*T*his part provides parliamentary procedures useful for any meeting. These are standard, universal rules based on commonly accepted practice in America. I have, however, made a few changes that I have found useful through the years, and these are noted and explained in the text. If you learn these rules, you will be able to preside over any meeting. There are a number of terms, such as *assembly, meeting, session, motion,* and *amendment,* on which you may need further clarification. The glossary contains an explanation of most of the terms used in parliamentary procedure.

CHAPTER 5

Governance Documents

*E*very organization should have at least two tiers of governance documents. The first, and superior, tier is a set of bylaws. This may be designated as "bylaws," a "constitution" or a "constitution with bylaws." A constitution and a set of bylaws are substantially the same thing. The second tier, which cannot conflict with the superior bylaws, is a set of standing rules which govern the conduct of the meetings of an organization. I will discuss each of these tiers in turn.

A third tier that is sometimes used is a charter, or articles of incorporation, which is filed with the Secretary of State under the provisions of the statutes for the appropriate state for voluntary, nonprofit organizations. Incorporation is particularly useful if the organization seeks tax exempt status with the Internal Revenue Service. Since articles of incorporation seldom impact upon the day-to-day operation of the organization, this subject is not discussed further in this book.

CONSTITUTION AND BYLAWS

Every organization should have one governance document that sets out the purpose of the organization, its membership requirements and structure, the rights of members, the powers and authority of its governance bodies, and the method for amending the document itself. This document, almost always somewhat difficult to amend, provides stability for the organization and security for the members, who invest in it their time, money, and energy.

Traditionally, organizations have used two such documents: a constitution and a set of bylaws. Each parallels the other in subjects covered, the basic difference between the two being the difficulty of amendment. Because the constitution is more difficult to amend than the bylaws, provisions essential to the goals and continuance of the organization are placed in the constitution; the correlated bylaws simply add more detail. For example, the constitution might provide for a board of directors and establish its broad powers and duties; the bylaws would add details on its organization and meetings. The constitution might provide for certain committees and authorize others "as provided for in the bylaws"; the bylaws would add housekeeping details for the standing committees and make necessary provisions for others.

The bylaws cannot conflict with the constitution, which is always the superior authority. If any conflict exists, the constitutional provisions prevail. Nor may provisions in either document be in conflict with national or state laws.

Organizations today frequently have only one document, usually called "bylaws." The advantage of a single document is obvious: a member does not have to consult two different documents or remember in which document a specific provision is to be found.

For purposes of this book, I will use the term *bylaws* to mean both types of governance documents.

Adoption of Bylaws

When bylaws are adopted for the first time by a new organization, the document, in its entirety, can be adopted by a simple majority vote. The reason is that, without the amending requirement of a two-thirds vote (contained in a document not yet adopted), the adopting assembly is subject to no other standard than the simple majority principle basic in parliamentary procedure generally. Once adopted, of course, the amending provisions contained in the document itself govern.

Amendments to Bylaws

Bylaws cannot be suspended. They cannot be amended without prior notice and a two-thirds vote. Details of these amendment requirements should be contained in the bylaws themselves. Most organizations also specify requirements for the submission of bylaw amendments so that a single member cannot initiate this formal process. Submission usually entails some formality, such as a petition signed by a given number of members or approval by the board of directors or by the committee on bylaws and rules.

A complete revision of the bylaws is a very special case, and the main motion, which is to adopt the entire new document, must be adopted by a two-thirds vote. The individual articles and sections of the proposed new bylaws, however, may be considered and voted upon one at a time and amended or adopted by a simple majority vote.

Once before the assembly, the proposed bylaw amendment is itself a main motion (that is, a free-standing, independent proposal), regardless of the name "amendment." It is handled exactly as a main motion and can be amended, or perfected, from the floor, without notice, by a simple majority vote, even though the main motion (the proposed bylaw amendment) requires a two-thirds vote for adoption.

There is an important requirement for floor amendments to proposed bylaw amendments: the floor amendment — made without notice — cannot enlarge upon or be more restrictive than the bylaw amendment for which notice was given. The reason for this requirement is to protect absentees. When notice of a bylaw amendment is given, all members have the right to rely on that notice and to know that, whether or not they attend the meeting, nothing can be adopted that is more drastic or more restrictive than the proposal for which they received notice. I sometimes explain it this way: the bylaw amendment cannot be advertised as a lamb before the meeting and then changed into a lion by a floor amendment at the meeting. The test is a bracketing process, best explained with an example of a proposed dues amendment. If the dues are set in the bylaws at $100 a year and a bylaw amendment increasing the dues to $120 is advertised in the notice to the members, then a floor amendment cannot attempt to set the dues at less than $100 (the status quo) or more than $120, the increase for which notice was given. In other words, $90 would be out of order, as would $125.

After some debate, it may appear to the assembly and the Chair that though the proposed bylaw amendment has some merit, it is not drafted properly and requires further study. In this case, the proposed bylaw amendment may be referred to a committee for consideration and redrafting, or it may be postponed to a later meeting with the understanding that improvements in the proposal will be made in the meantime. Before the proposed amendment is brought back before the assembly, proper notice should again be given to the members. (See pp. 105–106 for explanation of the motions to refer and to postpone.)

Bylaw amendments become effective immediately upon adoption unless the assembly has decided or clearly understands that the effective date is to be postponed. This postponement is usually achieved by prefatory language, such as "The effective date of this amendment, if adopted, shall be September 1 of this current year." The Chair should repeat this language before the vote is taken so the assembly clearly understands the effective date.

If it becomes clear to the Chair that the assembly is assuming an effective date other than immediately upon adoption, because of the content of the amendment, the Chair should state that, without objection, the later date will be the effective date. If there is objection, the assembly must vote on the question. A floor amendment that postpones the effective date may also be adopted. Bylaw amendments cannot be retroactive, but they can eliminate offices and make other substantial changes immediately upon their taking effect. For this reason, care should be taken as to the effective date.

For a model set of bylaws, see Appendix B. For references to sources containing more information on bylaws and their contents, consult the bibliography in this book.

STANDING RULES

The second tier of governance documents, the standing rules, contains provisions that relate to the actual conduct of the meetings of the organization, such as the meeting and the method for making, debating, and voting on motions — all the procedures necessary to fulfill the group's needs. If an organization has adopted a parliamentary procedure authority, such as this book or *Robert's*, in its bylaws, then its standing rules do not need to provide for anything except any rules that are different from or added to the standard rules provided by the authority.

When presented to the assembly for the very first time, standing rules may be adopted as the standing rules of the organization by a simple majority vote. After that adoption, standing rules should have some stability so that members can rely on them from meeting to meeting with few, if any, surprises. They can, however, be amended or suspended by a two-thirds vote *without* notice. For this reason, an organization should put such important matters as the requirement for a quorum or the amount of dues in the bylaws, and not in the standing rules. The test should be whether the provision could be changed or suspended without notice without risk to the organization. If there is no risk, then the provision can be in the standing rules. But if the provision is so important that it should not be suspended without notice, it should be a bylaw.

It is not wise to place housekeeping details, like meeting times and places, in the standing rules. Since most of these items change somewhat from year to year, their inclusion would mean that the standing rules would be under constant amendment and, as I have indicated, the members should not think of the standing rules as something so fluid and uncertain. The times of meetings, meeting rooms, and other such housekeeping items should simply be included in the notice of the meeting and the proposed agenda sent to members. Many organizations find that it is best to have an elected representative body, such as the board of directors, select the time and place of meetings of the assembly. A bylaw provision can place that responsibility with the appropriate governance body.

Set out in Appendix A is a model set of standing rules. These rules are obviously general to some extent and should be specifically designed to suit an organization's own practice and needs.

Amendments to Standing Rules

After the credentials committee's report has been adopted at a meeting as the first item of business, next on the agenda should be consideration of the standing rules.

If a proposed amendment to the standing rules has been previously received, the amendment should have been printed and distributed to the assembly. At the appropriate time, the Chair announces consideration of the standing rules and recognizes the chair of the rules committee. This person gives a report, if any, or presents the amendments received. The rules committee can recommend approval or rejection, or take no position at all. Another possible recommendation is for approval as amended by the committee. This report is handled like other committee reports.

Those amendments received but not recommended for approval and amendments from the floor proposed by a member can then be moved like any other main motion — that is, as an independent proposal put before the assembly for the first time.

The motion for amendment of the standing rules is a main motion and is not handled like an ordinary amendment. Because the bylaws and the standing rules are continuously in place, their adoption is not before the assembly. These governance documents have already been adopted. Therefore, an amendment to the standing rules is an original motion arising in the meeting and is a main motion.

A main motion amending the standing rules can be amended from the floor, and the floor amendment requires only a simple majority, even though the adoption of the main motion amending the standing rules requires a two-thirds vote. The logic for this approach is that a simple majority can perfect a proposed amendment, or get it into the form most acceptable to the assembly, but this perfecting process is not, in fact, amending the standing rules. Only the adoption of the main motion amendment — as perfected through floor amendment — is an amendment to the standing rules, which requires a two-thirds majority.

Suspension of the Standing Rules

It often occurs at some point in a meeting that the standing rules are interfering with the effective progress of the assembly's business. Then either the Chair will propose that the rules be suspended (usually, first put forward as a request for unanimous consent; see pp. 124–125) or a member may make a motion for suspension.

If the motion to suspend the standing rules is made only to facilitate a specific, immediate action that will not be repeated — for example, to allow a nonmember to speak before the assembly — the motion to suspend can incorporate the motion proposing the otherwise prohibited action. Although technically two motions are involved, a single, clearly worded motion will accomplish the same end more quickly and smoothly since motions to suspend the rules — and hence such composite motions — are not debatable. The wording of such composite motions should make their purpose clear to the assembly. In the example above, the Chair might restate the motion as "to suspend the rules and allow the speaker." If such a motion is questioned, the Chair can point out that it is not debatable but allow the proposing member to state the purpose of the motion. The purpose, however, as in the example above, is usually apparent in the wording of the motion. The motion is then put to a vote. It requires a two-thirds majority for adoption.

Another typical example of a combined motion is the motion to suspend the rules and reconsider all the resolutions previously adopted. This particular motion is called the "clincher" motion because its sponsor has the purpose of having the motion defeated. The motion to reconsider, once defeated, cannot be renewed. As a result, once this combined motion is defeated, all the resolutions previously adopted cannot be brought up again under any motion, and the sponsor, having "clinched" these votes, can be confident that those resolutions will not come before the assembly again in that meeting and that those issues are settled with finality. Under the normal rules, each vote on each resolution would have to be moved, debated, and then voted on individually; with all rules suspended, however, the reconsideration vote can be on all of the votes on all of the resolutions *en bloc* — all in this one combined motion. And since the motion to suspend the rules is not debatable, this combined motion is not debatable; all the earlier resolution votes, therefore, can be clinched in a matter of a few minutes.

Once suspended, the rules remain suspended only for the time indicated in the motion. For example, the organization's rules may set the time limit for individual speakers in debate at five minutes. The assembly suspends the rule in order to limit debate to two minutes for each speaker while considering some proposed resolutions. After the resolutions are completed, the regular rules come back into force. Similarly, the rules may be suspended for one meeting, in which case the regular standing rules are again in force at the next meeting.

Special Orders: A Suspension of Rules for a Specified Purpose

One of the more useful devices of the U.S. House of Representatives is the form of special orders. This form is not used in *Robert's* and, probably just for that reason, is not popular with most American writers on parliamentary procedure.

As used in the House of Representatives, a special order is a plan setting forth a detailed format for the consideration of and vote on a specific matter proposed by the House leadership or the sponsors of a particular bill. The special order is usually agreed to by unanimous consent because of earlier negotiations among the interested parties and the resulting compromises made to reach consensus. The details of a special order usually include the exact time when the debate is to begin, the limits of time for the whole debate, a division of the time between sides, the way that amendments will be handled (such as a limitation on the number of amendments), and an exact time for debate to end and the final vote to be taken on the main motion, as it may have been amended. The rules are suspended because the special order interrupts any other matter that might otherwise be before the body at that time and contains special rules of debate different from the usual House rules.

Obviously, this device is a great help to a body handling such a large volume of business as the U.S. Congress. But special orders can be helpful for any meeting at which a very important matter is to be considered and debated extensively and the members want to be certain there will be a final vote at an agreed-upon time. In this manner, more members can speak and all can plan according to the schedule. This form can set limits for each member's debate time, with speakers alternating for and against, or simply allocate a block of time (for example, thirty minutes) to each side, with an additional shorter period (for example, ten minutes) for each side to respond. Amendments may be limited in number for each side or prohibited altogether. Points of information may also be prohibited or limited in some way.

In short, special orders allow the assembly to custom-design a period of time for a debate and vote on an unusually important matter that would not be handled as well under the regular rules.

The usual motion is the combined motion to suspend the rules and adopt the proposed special order. Although the motion to suspend the rules is not amendable, more flexibility should be allowed if the Chair perceives that there is general agreement in principle but a difference of opinion on a detail of the proposed special order, such as the allotted time. The Chair, in this situation, can easily divide the question and allow the assembly to debate and amend the motion as to the time.

CHAPTER 6

Agenda

A basic step of any meeting, after the matter of credentials (see pp. 91–93) and consideration of standing rules, is adoption of the agenda. The agenda determines what business is to be considered at the meeting. It is the "road map" the members agree to follow from the beginning of the meeting to its end. Once the members agree to follow this specific route, it is relatively difficult for them to change the route later in the meeting.

Because the agenda controls the meeting, it is of the utmost importance. The agenda is first adopted by a simple majority vote. The members of the assembly are always technically in control of their agenda, but once they have adopted it, they can change it later only by a two-thirds vote.

The Chair customarily proposes the agenda as the next item of business after the credentials report has been adopted and any amendments to the standing rules have been considered. These three matters constitute the most basic and important decisions of the meeting: (1) the credentials report is a determination of the people legally in place as proper members of the assembly; (2) the standing rules and any amendments adopted are a determination by the properly seated members as to how they will conduct any business that comes before them; and (3) the agenda is their determination as to what they will do at this meeting within the time they have for it. The order is a logical sequence. There are reasons for putting the agenda this close to the beginning of the meeting: the first reason is to inform the members as soon as possible what to expect for the remainder of the meeting (they can be prepared for the substantive business and can be sure to be in their places when the items that interest them are presented); the second reason is to lock in the business of the meeting so that new or surprise items cannot be easily introduced, especially at the very end when a number of members may have left and the assembly is not then representative.

The next items on the agenda, after the initial three items, are what could be called items from management: reports from the president, the executive secretary, the treasurer, and any other officers. Then follow committee reports. After these institutionalized types of business come items not always on the agenda of every meeting: special committee reports, items of business for which members have given notice, and other such matters.

It is important to place items on the agenda in descending order of importance; if the meeting bogs down on some issues, all items may not be reached before someone moves for adjournment and the members vote to end the meeting.

Therefore, a recommended model agenda is as follows:

AGENDA

1. Call to order at ———— o'clock
2. Announcement of quorum
3. Credentials report (or a roll call in small meetings)
4. Adoption of rules (or presentation of any proposed amendments to standing rules if standing rules are already in place)
5. Adoption of the agenda
6. Report of the president
7. Report of other officers

8. Report of staff (such as the executive secretary or the general counsel)
9. Standing committee reports:
   a. Credentials committee (only if the first credentials report was an initial report and not the final report)
   b. Bylaws and rules committee
   c. Resolutions committee
   d. Budget and finance committee
   e. Elections committee
10. Reports of special committees
11. Specific items of business (such as items postponed from earlier meetings or items of business proposed by individual members)
12. Adjournment at ———— o'clock

The agenda need not include provisions for "old business" and "new business." Items of business postponed until a given meeting are the only old business that can properly come before that meeting, and they can be placed on the agenda as specific items like any other report or motion. *Do not include "new business" as an agenda item.* Calling for new business invites anyone to bring up anything at all. Even putting this category at the very end of the agenda, as some organizations customarily do, places at risk all the members' expectations of and planning for the meeting.

Advance notice of the intent to propose business at a meeting should be a procedural requirement. Such notice should be sent to the president (or other officer preparing the proposed agenda) for inclusion in the mailed notice of meeting sent to all members. Those who miss the deadline can seek to add items of business to the agenda by means of an amendment when it is considered at the beginning of the meeting.

The standing rules of each organization can set out a rule for notice of agenda items that best suits its own needs; there should always be some rule so that members will be aware of the procedure they should follow.

The NEA, for example, which holds four-day sessions, has

new business specified on its agenda, but the organization sets a deadline for prior written notice of each new-business item. These items are then reproduced and handed out to the delegates well before they are debated and voted on.

When all the business has been considered, the Chair may simply announce that all business having been concluded, the meeting is adjourned. Some meetings, however, continue on well beyond the time that most members had expected them to end. To provide for this contingency, it is well to include the item of adjournment and the time proposed for it in the agenda. This not only gives the members some idea of how long the meeting will last, it also affords the Chair the opportunity to initiate gracefully the question of adjournment. It can also be helpful in the opposite situation: if some members become restless before the business is completed and someone prematurely moves adjournment, the Chair can point out that the members had earlier decided to remain until a specified hour and thus gently urge the assembly to defeat the motion to adjourn.

The adoption of the agenda is handled like any other main motion. It is moved, usually by the secretary or some other officer, and then debated and possibly amended.

As I pointed out earlier, once adopted by the members of the assembly, the agenda is then the agreed-upon list of items of business for the remainder of the meeting, and this list cannot be changed (added to or reduced) except by a two-thirds vote of the assembly.

CHAPTER 7
Committees

The committee system is the most effective way for an organization to handle a number of diverse and complicated matters. A matter brought before the assembly may be referred to a committee for study and change; the committee later brings the matter back to a meeting of the organization for full consideration and possible final adoption. This procedure is often referred to as the "committee system."

TYPES OF COMMITTEES

Standing committees are those created in the governance document, usually the bylaws, as permanent committees. Typical standing committees are a budget committee, a bylaws and rules committee, and a resolutions committee. These standing committees often initiate their own recommendations in addition to receiving them from individual members or officers of the organization. The budget committee usually receives the proposed budget from the president or executive director and then reports a recommended budget to the assembly. Resolutions committees often receive proposed resolutions from individual members, edit them as to form and style, and report them to the assembly. The bylaws should specify the duties and powers of the resolutions committee so that it is clear that the committee must report out all resolutions submitted to it, even those the committee recommends for rejection. The assembly can then make its own decision as to whether it will follow the committee's recommendation. Without such a bylaw provision, the resolutions committee can easily become a resolutions graveyard.

Special committees, or ad hoc committees, are any that are not standing committees. They usually have a single-issue purpose, and a definite period of time is specified for their existence. The governance documents of some organizations designate certain committees as "standing" and authorize the board or assembly to create any needed additional committees. These additional committees may be as permanent and important as the bylaw-authorized standing committees. Thus, their name does not necessarily indicate their importance. The duties and powers delegated by the bylaws or the governance body, not the name, determine the role of a committee.

COMMITTEE MEETINGS

Committee meetings are governed by basically the same procedures as meetings of the assembly. Committees can be much more informal, however, and their chairs often initiate the matters to be considered and enter debate like any other member. There is no restriction on the number of times a member may speak. The quorum for a committee meeting is a majority of its members.

MINORITY REPORTS

Some organizations, such as the Democratic National Committee, provide for minority reports in their governance documents. At the Democratic National Convention, for example, if 20 percent of a committee signs (within certain time limits) a report that differs from the committee report, it is designated a "minority report." It is printed along with the committee report and receives preference in recognition after the committee report has been moved for adoption, both substantial advantages for a minority position.

A member who supports the committee report may not also sign the minority report, though members are given some time to change their minds about signing. Allowing a member to be counted both ways would frustrate a rule such as the Democratic National Convention's 20 percent rule.

If there is no particular rule governing minority reports, any member or group of members of the committee may at any time put together an alternative to the committee report and propose it from the floor as an amendment to that report. But in this situation, there is no preference as to recognition — minority members must seek recognition from the Chair like any other member wishing to speak — nor does this type of minority report have to be included with the distributed committee report. Thus, the advantages of a formal minority report are lost.

ADOPTION OF A COMMITTEE REPORT

The Chair calls on the committee chair to make the committee report. That person usually makes a statement, the length of which, of course, depends on the complexity and importance of the report. If possible, written copies of the report have already been distributed to the assembly. The committee chair then moves, on behalf of the committee, the adoption of the report. Because the report necessarily has the support of more than one member, there is no need for a second.

The report itself usually contains a narrative description of the purpose, objectives, and work of the committee and concludes with specific recommendations. When the report is moved for adoption, only the recommendations are at issue. What the committee actually did in its work is now history and cannot be changed. But the recommendations the committee wants the assembly to adopt are subject to all the motions of any main motion — amendment, postponement, referral back to the committee for further study, and adoption or rejection.

DEBATE ON A COMMITTEE REPORT

If an amendment to the report is moved from the floor, the maker of the motion has preference in recognition to speak to the amendment as with any other motion. The committee chair has preference to respond. If the entire committee is present with the chair, as is sometimes the case in larger meetings, the committee can take a quick caucus at the podium and authorize its chair to accept an amendment as a "friendly amendment." (See p. 104 for a description of "friendly amendment.") The committee chair cannot otherwise accept amendments on behalf of the committee.

Often, when the amendment is obviously friendly in nature, the committee chair will state that, though it is not possible to speak for the committee that is not there assembled as a committee, the committee chair is confident that the committee would not object to the floor amendment. In that case, the assembly Chair seeks unanimous consent, and if there is no objection, the floor amendment is adopted as the "friendly amendment" would have been adopted. Presumably, the members of the committee are among the members on the floor and did not object when the Chair gave all members present the opportunity to object. If the amendment is not accepted as friendly, it is handled like any other amendment.

Committees, then, are the "worker bees" of the organization, doing much detailed and time-consuming work in order to present as thoughtful and as practicable a proposal as possible for consideration and adoption by the full assembly.

CHAPTER 8

Preliminaries

*T*he preliminaries are those actions that take place before the meeting actually begins its business. They include giving notice of the meeting: informing the members that a meeting will be held, the place, and the time; establishing a quorum: confirming that enough members are in attendance so that the action taken is representative of the total membership; and ascertaining credentials: making certain that only those people who are eligible members are present and voting on the business.

NOTICE OF THE MEETING

Written notice of the meeting, along with the proposed agenda, should be mailed to each member within a reasonable time prior to the meeting. In organizations that have periodic general mailings, such as a monthly newsletter or journal, the notice and proposed agenda can be published in the periodical. Such notice is reasonable and essential to fair play. A clandestine meeting, with only a few members being informed of it, is obviously contrary to both parliamentary procedure and democratic practice.

Courts of law have shown a consistent reluctance to intervene in the actions of meetings of private organizations. They do so only in cases of obvious fraud. A threshold question the court will ask in the event of a legal challenge is, did all members receive reasonable notice? If they were not adequately notified, there arises a presumption of lack of due process.

The notice should clearly state the time and place of the meeting and should be sent well in advance so that all members have time enough to prepare themselves for the meeting. There is no established standard concerning the amount of time required for proper notice. Each organization determines what best fits its needs. Seven days' notice is appropriate in cases of assemblies that meet regularly, say, monthly or quarterly. But national groups that convene annually or every two or four years require much more notice. Also, the sort of business the assembly will address should be considered. Seven days' notice is reasonable for routine business but thirty days' notice would be more reasonable if an assembly will be considering an extensively altered set of bylaws. Commonsense should indicate how much time would be required for average members to receive the materials and review them thoroughly. They should have sufficient time to understand any issues involved, since they may not be as focused on a matter as the officers or other interested parties. They should never have to complain at a meeting that they didn't have enough time to consider something they are required to vote on.

If the meeting is designated a "special meeting" — that is, a meeting that is not regularly scheduled but is called to deal with a specific issue or item of business — the notice should state that purpose. At a special meeting, the assembly cannot consider anything other than the issue or item of business specified in the notice. This rule governing special meetings cannot be suspended to consider additional items of business because the rule requiring proper notice cannot be suspended.

The proposed agenda is an essential part of the notice sent to members. They need to know what to expect when they attend or what they will miss if they do not. The protection of the rights of absentees is a fundamental principle of parliamentary procedure.

The standing rules of the organization may require that the full text of any substantive motion, other than floor amendments, be placed in the proposed agenda. The full text is recommended. If that is not considered necessary, the organization should, at a minimum, require advance notice of what the officer who prepares the agenda knows will come before the meeting. And, at the beginning of the meeting when the agenda is up for adoption, all members should be required to come forward with notice of their substantive motions, so all will know what to expect.

As noted in *Palgrave*, a traditional British manual of procedures, "Where there is no rule, equity demands that no member should be placed at a disadvantage by being confronted with unexpected decisions on matters of importance" (1964, p. 57).

QUORUM

A quorum is the minimum number of members required to be present at a meeting in order for business to be acted upon. Without a quorum, the meeting cannot proceed with any business, except to recess while taking steps to obtain a quorum or to adjourn.

The bylaws of the organization should set the quorum at the reasonable number of members who can be expected to attend. Each organization must make that determination according to its own requirements. Thus, it could be reasonable in some special circumstances to have a quorum consisting of only 25 percent of the total membership or a specific number, such as fifteen, when the total membership is sixty.

In the absence of a bylaw provision, a quorum is considered to be a majority of the total membership. In a convention made up of delegates representing members, a quorum is a majority of the delegates who actually register and are seated by the credentials committee and the assembly (as opposed to all those authorized to attend). The quorum for a committee or a board is a majority of the total number of members of the committee or board.

The requirement of a quorum to do business is based on the policy that it is not wise to have a very small minority of the members taking action for the whole organization, unless, through the bylaws, the members have agreed to allow a number smaller than a majority to act for them.

When the Chair calls the meeting to order, the Chair is, by that act, declaring that a quorum is present. Some Chairs like to make a specific announcement of the presence of a quorum; if a verbatim transcript is kept and there is some chance of legal challenge to any part of the meeting, it is recommended that the Chair announce the presence of a quorum for the record.

The Chair has a duty to avoid taking action on business when it is clear that, because some members have left, a quorum no longer exists. If members are simply out in the halls, the Chair can request that someone go out and ask the members to return. If after a reasonable time they have not returned in sufficient numbers to reestablish a quorum, the Chair should adjourn the meeting.

If a member believes that a quorum has been lost, a point of order can be made and the Chair must then rule on the presence of a quorum. A member who believes the Chair's ruling is incorrect can appeal it. In highly contested situations, a majority of the members can persist in challenging the Chair's determination of the vote on appeal and demand a counted vote, with abstentions also recorded. The counted vote will automatically provide an accurate determination of the number of members present for purposes of determining a quorum.

Although the requirement of a quorum can appear to be a technicality of little importance, it can become an effective weapon in cases in which a minority cannot control the votes but can leave the meeting, causing the loss of a quorum and thus preventing any further action by the assembly.

CREDENTIALS

A basic decision of any assembly is deciding who is properly there as a member for that meeting. If there is any doubt as to the status of members present and voting, all actions of the assembly become suspect.

Most organizations have little difficulty in making this determination. Small groups that meet regularly do not use a credentials committee but simply call the roll or, more often, observe the members present and see that they are, in fact, those who should be in attendance.

For larger meetings, such as a national convention of delegates, a credentials committee is selected well in advance, and this committee reviews the registration of each member attending. Any challenge concerning the seating of a delegate is brought before the committee, which considers it and decides who should be seated. This committee then prepares a list, or "roll of delegates," which contains the name of each member the committee has determined is eligible to attend. The committee then goes before the assembly and moves adoption of its credentials committee report, which, if adopted, seats the named delegates.

If the registration of delegates continues after the hour set for the first meeting of the assembly to begin, most organizations receive a preliminary report from the credentials committee that lists only those delegates who have registered up to that time. The number contained in this report fixes the quorum requirement (based on one-half of the delegates actually registered as attending) until a later report is made that contains the final count of registered delegates on the close of registration.

A logical question arises as to how the Chair can declare a quorum before the credentials committee has reported. By practice, large meetings rely upon the visual estimate of the Chair on the assumption that those present are good-faith, legal members. The later report of the credentials committee can change that assumption, and the Chair would have to rule on the presence or absence of a quorum based on this later report. In smaller meetings, there is often a roll call, which establishes both the legality of those attending and the number present for purposes of a quorum.

Challenges to the Seating of a Member

The first step to the challenge of the seating of a delegate is an appearance before the credentials committee, which evaluates the facts. After a careful investigation, the committee makes the determination.

When the report of the credentials committee is before the assembly, any member who still wishes to challenge the seating of someone can do so by moving an amendment from the floor. This amendment is handled like any other. (See pp. 103–105.) It can seek to add names to the list or subtract them or delete some names and add others in their place.

In voting on a challenge, such as a floor amendment, those delegates who are being challenged cannot vote on their own challenge. But this rule does not extend to a whole delegation, so that if, for example, the only delegates for a state being challenged are from a particular district, then only those from that district are excluded from the vote; the remaining delegates from that state can vote on the challenge.

Upon the final adoption of the credentials committee's report, the assembly has made a final determination, and those members whose names are then on the list (in the main motion, with amendments, if any) are properly seated. The assembly is the final judge of the seating of its members for that meeting. There is no further appeal.

Sometimes the question arises as to the legality of seating certain members when it is fairly clear that the bylaws, which limit the number of delegates from a given geographic area, are being violated. Customarily, the will of the assembly prevails on the theory that, at some point, only a political compromise will allow the meeting to go forward, regardless of the specific requirements of the bylaws. For example, a political convention might choose to seat two competing groups in a state's delegation, even though that move would create more than the number of delegates to which the state was originally entitled.

National conventions of the two major political parties have often found that the adoption of the credentials committee report was the most critical vote in the convention and, in fact, determined the final outcome of the nomination of their candidates.

Alternates

Many organizations that provide for annual or less frequent meetings elect alternates for delegates who fail to attend or who leave the meeting before it is over, for whatever reason. The governance provisions of some organizations stipulate that an alternate, once seated, may continue to have the seat of the original delegate, even though that person subsequently returns to the floor. In other governance provisions, the alternate is only temporary and has to give up the seat if the original delegate returns.

An alternate who has taken the place of a delegate exercises all the power and has all the duties of the original delegate. For that reason, an alternate must meet the same standards and requirements as the original delegate and should be elected carefully under the same rules.

CHAPTER 9

Motions

A matter requiring the decision of the House of Commons is decided by means of a question put from the Chair upon a motion made by a member. . . .

A motion is a proposal made for the purpose of eliciting a decision of the House.
— May, *Parliamentary Practice*, p. 321

A matter requiring a decision of the assembly is initiated by means of a motion made by a member. The five steps are the motion moved by a member; the motion stated to the assembly and proposed as a question by the Chair; debate of the question; the putting of the question by the Chair for a vote; and the determination of the votes for and against the motion.

A motion is stated and put by the Chair as a simple question so that members of the assembly can vote either yes or no. There are no in-between positions. If some members are neither for nor against the motion as it is put by the Chair, they must attempt to change (amend) the motion or otherwise dispose of it. Or they can *abstain*, which means they do not vote at all.

Motions are either substantive or procedural. Many writers have devised elaborate categories that include such terms as "subsidiary," "ancillary," and "incidental." It is easier just to be aware of what different motions do, so that such category names become unnecessary.

When a new, independent proposal is first put before the assembly in the form of a motion, it is a *substantive motion* and is called a *main motion*. Main motions usually propose that the organization take some action or position on a matter. Often, the motion concerning a position is written in the form of a resolution, with prefatory clauses known as "whereas" clauses, followed by "now, therefore . . ." and affirmation clauses, although the modern trend in resolution drafting drops the "whereas" clause form and utilizes more informal, direct wording.

A procedural motion is, as its name indicates, a motion that affects the procedure to be followed by the assembly upon its adoption. One of the most frequently used procedural motions is the motion to close debate. Once adopted, the members have agreed that the *debate* procedure *has ended* and (the next step in the process) *voting shall begin*. Another typical example is the motion to refer. Once adopted, this motion *sends* the matter then before the assembly to whatever body is specified in the motion, such as the resolutions committee. In this manner, procedural motions always contain as their prime element some action on the part of the assembly: to close debate, to refer, to postpone, to suspend the rules, to reconsider (that is, to go back to an earlier vote), to adjourn.

A motion should always be stated in the affirmative, not the negative, because, when the question is put for a vote, the Chair asks for ayes and noes. If the motion were in the negative, members could become confused as to which way to vote — an aye vote would be negative and a no vote affirmative.

THE TWELVE BASIC MOTIONS

There are twelve basic functions in parliamentary procedure with twelve corresponding motions. Many authorities employ many more motions; *Robert's,* as I've said, lists eighty-four. Many of these additional motions, however, are no more than variations on a basic motion, utilized by some writers and parliamentarians in order to have a more specialized or descriptive language for a special function that is included in the basic function. For example, the basic motion to postpone has the function of delaying action on a pending main motion. Variations of this motion are to postpone to a certain time and to table. Although these variations have different characteristics and results, they nevertheless share the basic functions of delaying action. In this book, I use only one motion for delaying — the basic motion to postpone. In some other case, the functions are exactly the same; only the name is different, as in the motion to close debate and the motion to move the previous question.

See the table on pages 98–99, which lists the twelve basic motions and the most common variations of each.

It is not improper to use some of the variations, but they are not necessary as additional motions. Some of them, such as the motions to table and to object to consideration, are not consistent with other goals of basic parliamentary procedure and should not be used. Basic parliamentary procedure does not allow a restriction on the right of a member to speak, except by a two-thirds vote; the motion to table cuts off debate by a simple majority. Basic parliamentary procedure allows every member to speak, even though that member is very much in the minority; the motion to object to consideration, if sustained, can prohibit a member from speaking at all. Interestingly, these two troublesome motions do not have their roots in the British Parliament, as do most motions, but are relatively recent American innovations.

Presiding officers uncertain which motions both require a two-thirds vote and are not debatable need remember that only two motions on this short list have these characteristics: the motion to suspend the rules and the motion to close debate. Both relate to the right of the members to speak under the standing rules of the organization.

PROCEDURAL REQUIREMENTS

Although the following discussion relates specifically to the procedural requirements for a main motion — the workhorse of any meeting — these procedural requirements apply generally to all the basic motions. Exceptions will be noted elsewhere when a particular motion is discussed.

Basic Motion	Debatable	Vote Required	Amendable	See page:
Main Motion	Yes	Majority	Yes	97–103
Amend	Yes	Majority	Yes	103
Postpone (to a certain time)	Yes	Majority	Yes	105
Refer	Yes	Majority	Yes	105
Close Debate	No	2/3	No	109
Divide the Question	Yes	Majority	Yes	112
Motions Relating to Voting	No	Majority (except for divisions and roll call votes)	No	112
Reconsider	Yes	See comments	No	126
Request (to the assembly to allow something)	No	Majority	No	111
Suspend the Rules	No	2/3	No	75
Appeal	Yes	Majority	No	115
Adjourn	No	Majority	No, but see comments	136

Variation of Basic Motion	Comments
Adopt/Approve/Accept/Agree to	These four variations of wording for the main motion are interchangeable.
Add, or insert Delete, or strike out Substitute, or delete and add in lieu of	Any form that seeks to change the main motion is a motion to amend.
Postpone indefinitely Table	The motions "postpone indefinitely" and "table" should not be used.
Commit Recommit	The motion "commit" is restricted to referring a matter to a committee.
Move the previous question Move the question Call the question	All three variations using the word "question" mean to close debate and should not be used since they can be confusing.
	Allowed only when the question contains two or more independent matters.
Division (a standing vote or show of hands) Counted vote (roll call vote) Secret ballot, or written ballot Close nominations Close or reopen polls	A single member may demand a division. A roll call vote should require a 1/3 vote. All other motions should require a simple majority vote.
Rescind	A simple majority vote if the motion is made on the same day or the next day after the matter to be reconsidered was voted upon, or if notice of the motion has been given; otherwise a 2/3 vote is required.
Withdraw a motion Allow a nonmember to speak Dispense with the reading of the minutes (and approve them) Any request that does not require a suspension of the rules	The maker of a motion may withdraw the motion without a request if it is withdrawn prior to the Chair's stating the motion.
Limit or extend debate Amend the agenda after its adoption Take a matter out of its order on the agenda Adopt a special order of business Objection to consideration Any request that requires a suspension of the rules	Any motion that alters the usual right of members to speak requires a suspension of the rules. This motion can also include another motion, such as to suspend the rules and reconsider the adoption of the budget, in which case the motion to reconsider becomes undebatable.
	A tie vote or less than a majority vote causes the appeal to fail.
Recess	A recess is a brief adjournment. Although not usually amendable, if the motion contains a time to reconvene, it may be amended as to the time.

Notice of Motions

The organization's standing rules should require advance written notice of all substantive motions, except amendments, and even amendments of any complexity should have advance notice, if possible. This notice should be the complete written text of the motion, which is included in the mailing of the notice of meeting and the proposed agenda to all members and also in any printed publication, such as the monthly journal of the organization. Members do not like surprises; they want to understand what they are being asked to vote on. Of course, there are times in highly contested matters when surprise and uncertainty are used as weapons, but it should be clearly understood that these tactics are negative weapons — effective, perhaps, but nevertheless negative.

Written Motions

The greatest risk to any motion is that it will not be understood and therefore will be voted down. To avoid this, all motions of any length, no matter how large or small the meeting, should be in writing. As I recommended above, the preferred process for distribution of this written motion is to include it in the mailing of the notice of meeting and the proposed agenda to all members, as well as in any published notice. If there is not time for this process, such as during the meeting itself, then the member should come to the meeting with enough printed copies for distribution to all members at the appropriate time.

Very large assemblies, such as the annual NEA conventions, recognize the practical problem of having printed copies of these items, such as floor amendments not included in the notice of meeting, distributed to thousands of delegates. To delay the meeting while copies are printed and distributed is not feasible. Therefore, the NEA has developed an amazingly efficient process by which a written proposal, such as a floor amendment, can be transcribed into a closed-circuit television system and the text shown on a large overhead screen above the podium. The process obviously requires some lead time for the transcribing, but an alert member can file the text and it will be ready within minutes rather than hours.

Making the Motion

The member rises, obtains recognition from the Chair, and, with no other statement, makes the motion. Although the Chair can consider any form of a proposal to be the moving of a motion, the member is best served by using the words "I move . . ." so that there can be no question that a motion is being made. The mover cannot speak to the motion until it has been seconded and stated by the Chair.

Seconding the Motion

There is no absolute requirement for a second. (In fact, the British House of Commons has dropped the requirement altogether.) The theory behind compelling one is that the assembly should not be subjected to motions that have the support of only one member. In those cases in which the Chair believes that the maker is the only supporter of the motion, the Chair can ask for a second and, if none comes forward, announce that the motion "dies for lack of a second."

Even if there is no second, once a motion is stated by the Chair and debate has begun, the Chair has, in effect, ruled that there is apparent support for the motion and that a formal second is unnecessary. If the Chair's assumption is challenged, the quickest and easiest move is for the Chair simply to ask if there is a second. If debate has already progressed to the point that both the maker and another member have spoken in support of the motion, the Chair can respond to a challenge by pointing out that there is obvious support for the motion from a second member.

If an organization has a well-established custom of seconds, then the seconder should be recognized, since in any event it does no harm. The maker receives preference in speaking to the motion, but the seconder does not; so allowing a second usually requires only a few minutes of time, if that is a consideration.

A motion from a committee, such as a motion to adopt its report, is automatically seconded since a committee has more than one member; another second is not needed.

Statement of the Motion by the Chair

The stating of the motion by the Chair is no mere formality. In stating the motion, the Chair is actually ruling that it is in order — that is, that the motion is not contrary to the governance documents of the organization, is not contrary to law, and is otherwise appropriately brought before the assembly. If any member does not believe that the motion is in order, this is the best time to make the challenge — although the motion can be challenged as not being in order at any time before it is voted on.

The Chair also uses this opportunity to make sure the wording of the motion is in such form that it is well understood by the assembly. For example, if the motion should happen to be worded in the negative, the Chair can ask the maker to change it to an affirmative statement. Or should it contain minor errors as to names, dates, or similar items, the Chair can ask the mover to make those corrections before the motion is stated by the Chair. If the mover agrees, those changes can be made informally by unanimous consent. As pointed out earlier, to have the written text in the hands of the Chair and all members makes this process much easier and more certain.

Once stated by the Chair, the motion becomes the property of the assembly, and it no longer belongs to the maker. It is then the "pending motion." The motion as it is restated by the Chair prevails in the event that there is any difference between the wording of the maker and the wording by the Chair. The Chair may be making slight changes in order for the motion to be in order. If the maker disagrees with the Chair's restatement of the motion, then the maker must object at that time or be bound by the Chair's restatement.

Withdrawal of Motions

Before the Chair states the motion, the maker may withdraw the motion without approval from the seconder or the assembly.

For example, the Chair might point out to the maker that the proposed motion is unnecessary because of previous action, and the maker could then simply withdraw it.

But once stated by the Chair, the maker must obtain the consent of the assembly for withdrawal. The usual procedure is for the maker to request withdrawal and the Chair to ask for unanimous consent for withdrawal. If there is an objection, then the Chair, with no debate, puts the question as to whether the maker may withdraw the motion, and the assembly decides by a majority vote.

AMENDMENTS

An amendment is a substantive motion that seeks to change the main motion by one of three means: (1) by adding (the same as inserting), (2) by deleting (the same as striking), or (3) by first deleting and then adding (the same as substituting in lieu thereof).

An amendment to an amendment (called an amendment to the second degree) is used when there is support for an amendment, but some members wish to change (perfect) it before it is voted on. Purely as a practical matter, to avoid confusion, there can be no amendment proposed to a second-degree amendment. If the second-degree amendment needs change, it should be voted on first; after it has become a part of the first amendment, it can be further amended.

An amendment is handled generally like any other motion. That is, the member moves the motion, there is a second (if that is the custom), the Chair states the motion, debate follows, and the Chair puts the question on the amendment and takes the vote.

There may be a temptation for the Chair to stop after an amendment is either adopted or defeated. This feeling arises sometimes when an amendment involves a critical battle between two somewhat evenly divided vocal groups in the assembly. As debate progresses, it becomes clear that there are two clear-cut positions: the main motion or the amendment. The Chair must nevertheless continue the debate on the main motion either as it has been amended or as originally proposed without amendment. There is a very important reason for this procedure. For example, say the main motion is to send delegates, at their own expense, to a special conference. The amendment seeks to substitute a provision giving the delegates full travel expenses. After the Chair has taken the vote on the amendment, regardless of the outcome, the Chair must still put the vote on the main motion because the assembly may want to defeat the main motion on the ground that it simply opposes sending delegates to the conference with or without expenses.

It is not unusual for a floor amendment to be proposed that is acceptable to the sponsor of the main motion. A Chair who senses this to be the case can state the question of the floor amendment but then recognize the sponsor and ask if the sponsor would accept it as a "friendly amendment." If the sponsor agrees, the Chair (without recognizing the maker of the floor amendment) asks the entire assembly if the proposed floor amendment is acceptable "without objection." This procedure in effect asks the assembly to vote immediately on the floor amendment, without debate, but only the no votes are called for.

The usual script is as follows:

Chair: Is there objection to accepting this proposed amendment as part of the main motion?

(The Chair pauses and listens for any objection voiced by a member.)

Chair: Hearing no objection, this amendment has been adopted by unanimous consent, and I shall recognize the next speaker.

If there is objection, but by only a very few members, the Chair can still immediately put the question on the amendment without debate. If there is substantial objection, however, such as 10 to 20 percent of the members, then the Chair should go back to the sponsor of the floor amendment and use the same procedure as though the amendment were not friendly or acceptable to the maker of the main motion. (See pp. 124–125, "Decisions by Unanimous Consent.")

An amendment may be hostile to the motion it seeks to amend — that is, it can be contrary to the purposes and principles of the motion — but it should not simply negate it. For example, the amendment cannot simply add the word *not* to the motion or delete all the words after the "whereas" clause in a resolution. The Chair should refuse to take such an amendment and advise the member proposing it that the proper way to defeat the main motion is simply to vote against it.

OTHER DISPOSITION OF MOTIONS

In addition to amending, the assembly can take two other basic courses of action on any pending main motion by moving either to postpone it or to refer it.

Postponement of a Motion

The procedural motion to postpone is handled like any other motion except, of course, that it must be made while a main motion is pending. If any amendments are also pending at the time, the motion to postpone includes both the main motion and the amendments.

The postponement motion should either set a specific or certain time to which the matter is to be postponed or state what has to happen before the matter is to be brought up again — such as "immediately after the budget has been adopted." The postponement may be to a time later during the same meeting or to a later meeting. If to a later meeting, the postponed item is automatically placed on the proposed agenda included in the written notice of that meeting sent to the members.

The Chair should not take a motion to postpone indefinitely, for this motion does no more than negate the main motion in much the same way that the amendment to add the word *not* negates it. Neither motion serves any real purpose. The proper way to defeat a main motion is to vote against it.

Referral of a Motion

A main motion, and any pending amendments, can also be referred, and this, too, is handled like any other motion.

This procedural motion can vary widely, depending on the purpose of the referral. The two basic variations are (1) it states to whom the main motion is referred (such as the president, another officer, a committee, or the board of directors), and (2) it includes instructions for the recipient.

Instructions tell the recipient of the referral what to do with the item: for example, consider it and report back to the next meeting; or seek legal counsel and determine the best course of action for the organization; or redraft the item into a better considered and written proposal and report it at the next meeting.

CHAPTER 10

Debate

Debate is the lifeblood of any meeting — the interest, the excitement, the battle — with members matching their ideas and skills. In theory, the Chair is not a part of the debate at all. But in reality, the Chair is the most important factor in providing good, constructive, and fair debate.

PRECEDENCE IN RECOGNITION

The maker of a motion, as already mentioned, is the first to be recognized by the Chair to speak. The seconder does not have preference, except by special rule. The Chair seeks to recognize members after the maker in alternating order, for and against the motion. But there are other purposes for which a member may seek recognition that take precedence and interrupt the for-and-against order.

If a point of order is the purpose, that member is recognized as soon as possible. Some practices even allow for interruption of a speaker. If the Chair believes that the point of order, if correct, would obviate the speech of the member then speaking, the Chair should ask the speaker to defer so that the challenging member can present the point of order.

A member who wishes to ask a question concerning the motion before the assembly is also given preference in the order of recognition; but in this case, the Chair should not interrupt the speaker even though the question might be germane. It is better to ask the questioning member to wait until the current speaker has finished.

DEBATE PROCEDURE

Once the motion is made and seconded and has been stated by the Chair, the floor is open for debate. All debate and communication involving members must be through the Chair — that is, the Chair recognizes the member, and the member addresses the Chair. If someone wishes to ask another member a question, the person addresses the Chair and asks the question; the Chair, in turn, calls on the other person to respond. Questions to the chair of a committee proposing a report are handled the same way.

The Chair should insist this procedure be followed from the beginning of debate. Though the process may seem somewhat formal with purely routine matters, it becomes absolutely necessary when controversial issues arise, and the debate becomes heated. So the Chair should set the pattern of control on all matters from the beginning.

TIME AND NUMBER OF SPEECHES
IN DEBATE

The standing rules should designate a time limit for speeches by members in debate. In large conventions, the limit may be two minutes for individual members speaking as such and three minutes for those speaking as official representatives of a delegation in the convention.

If there is no rule, the accepted limit is ten minutes. But, except under the most unusual circumstances, ten minutes is too long if members have received notice and written motions. Therefore, it is desirable to have a time limit specifically designed for the organization in the standing rules.

The time required to ask or answer a question is not counted as time in debate.

A member may not speak more than twice on any one issue and cannot speak the second time until all who wish to speak on the same side of the issue have done so.

CLOSING DEBATE

When the Chair judges that members on both sides of a question have had ample opportunity to debate the issue and that the debate has been both substantial and commensurate with the importance of the question, the Chair should initiate steps to close debate. The Chair cannot actually close debate, however; only the assembly can. But the Chair can, for example, suggest to the assembly that, in the Chair's judgment, both sides have been heard and that after two more speakers are heard, one on each side, the Chair intends to put the question. Or the Chair might observe that the only remaining speakers are all on one side of the question and that if no member seeks recognition to speak on the other side, the Chair will put the question after the next speaker.

If this proposal elicits some resistance, but only a little, the question of closing debate can be proposed as a formal motion by the Chair. On the other hand, if there is general resistance, the Chair should announce that debate will continue until a member moves the question of closing debate.

This process of the Chair's taking steps to close debate is obviously a matter of judgment and timing. The same process may not be appropriate in all cases, as, for example, when a motion is of great importance to the members.

Remember: in order to avoid confusion, the Chair should always use the same simple words for this motion: "to close debate." If a member uses the term "previous question" in a motion, then the Chair should restate the motion for the assembly: "The question is, shall we close debate?" (See pp. 24–25.)

The motion to close debate is not debatable and requires a two-thirds vote for adoption.

CHAPTER 11

Initiatives from the Floor

*A*lthough rank-and-file members in the meeting are usually restricted to debate and voting on motions put by the Chair and in elections, they nevertheless have a few opportunities to raise matters on their own initiative. These initiatives fall into the four categories discussed in this chapter.

REQUESTS FROM THE ASSEMBLY

There are a number of different requests that a member may make from the floor. Some are on the member's own initiative (see Motion to Divide the Question and Motions Relating to Voting, pp. 112–113); others are in response to an invitation from the Chair. Among the latter, one of the most common is the Chair's question, "Shall the secretary read the minutes?" Usually someone responds by moving that the minutes not be read but be approved as printed and mailed to the members.

The request requires a simple majority vote and is usually

not debated, although in the case of the minutes, if they contain an error, there can be an amendment to make the correction before they are approved.

Another example is a request for withdrawal. The maker of a motion may request its withdrawal at any time before it is voted on. The Chair customarily asks for unanimous consent (without objection) for withdrawal. If there is any objection, the request of the maker is treated like any other simple request and the Chair puts the question to the assembly.

If a member wishes to have a nonmember speak to the assembly and there is no rule prohibiting it, then the motion to allow it is treated simply as a request. (But if the organization has a rule prohibiting nonmembers from speaking, then, as already discussed, there must be a motion to suspend the rules, and this requires a two-thirds majority vote.) Of course, many nonmembers come before meetings when the agenda includes outside speakers or reports from various specialists. Customarily the assembly does not vote on whether to allow these nonmembers to speak, but if there were an objection, the assembly would make its decision on the basis of a request made by a member.

In short, a request is any motion by a member that does not go against the organization's rules and does not, therefore, require a suspension of the rules.

MOTION TO DIVIDE THE QUESTION AND MOTIONS RELATING TO VOTING

If the motion to be voted on, usually the main motion, contains two or more matters that could stand independently if separated from the others, a member may propose that the question (that is, the motion) be divided. The request for a division may be for purposes of both debate and vote on the separate matters or for purposes of the vote only. For the better protection of the assembly, I advocate requiring a majority vote of the assembly to divide the question, rather than allowing a single member to do so, as is allowed in some other guides. (See pp. 125–126.)

Individual members may initiate a number of motions relating to voting, from the request for a division of the assembly (a standing vote or a show of hands) to a counted vote to a roll call vote. These motions are discussed in detail in the section on voting (see pp. 120–124).

POINTS OF INFORMATION

A point of information is a question from a member relating to a motion before the assembly and is directed either to the Chair or through the Chair to the member sponsoring the motion. A point of information takes precedence in recognition in the usual speaking order on the theory that members need their questions answered before they are required to vote on an issue. Even after debate is closed, questions may still be asked and answered.

The Chair must use a strict hand to make certain that questions are succinctly stated and are indeed made for the purpose of obtaining information, not for the purpose of debate. Rhetorical questions will sometimes arise, and if the Chair allows them, some members may try to take over the debate process. For example, assume that the assembly has adopted something like a colored-card system for recognition, and a member realizes there are many others ahead in the order of recognition of speakers. The person calls for a point of information, but then asks a rhetorical question — a thinly disguised way of moving ahead in the speaking-order line and entering the debate. A firm hand by the Chair is the only solution, and the offending member should be interrupted immediately and ruled out of order.

PARLIAMENTARY INQUIRIES

A parliamentary inquiry is similar to a point of information except that it is always a question concerning procedure and is always directed to the Chair. The member might ask, for example, why a current procedure is being used or whether it is being properly followed, or might suggest that another procedure would be more appropriate. Hypothetical questions are out of order. A member can appeal the Chair's decision if the member believes strongly that the Chair is in error — in effect, demanding that the Chair follow another procedure suggested by the member and asking the assembly to vote on the issue.

A member can raise the same type of question on a point of order, and the two initiatives in effect are the same. Obviously, the parliamentary inquiry is a more tactful way to ask a question, for the point of order is a direct challenge that the Chair is procedurally in error.

Points of Order

If any member believes, in good faith, that the rules of the organization (such as time limits on debates) or general parliamentary procedural rules (such as the requirement that a floor amendment be relevant to the motion it seeks to amend) are being violated, the member may seek recognition for the purpose of raising a point of order.

Once recognized, the member raises the point, and the Chair considers it and makes a ruling. It makes no difference how the Chair phrases this response; it is considered a ruling. For example, say the point of order concerns a floor amendment that is challenged as being out of order because it is not relevant. The Chair can rule that it is relevant or simply say that the Chair is not in agreement and ask the debate to proceed. Whatever the form, it is apparent that the Chair has made a ruling. This statement or action can be appealed to the assembly if the challenging member believes the ruling is incorrect.

As in the case of the misuse of points of information, a member may seek a point of order only to make a speech for or against a motion. Again, the person may be at the back of the line in the order of recognition of speakers, so he or she seeks a point of order to move to the front. The Chair's being firm and fair is absolutely essential in this situation. If a member recognized on a point of order begins a substantive speech, the Chair must interrupt and inform the member that recognition was for the sole purpose of a point of order and ask, "What rule of procedure are we now violating?" If the member does not immediately state a point of order based on the violation of a rule, the Chair should demand that the member be seated.

Appeals

Though the Chair has by far the greatest opportunity for exercising power and control in a meeting, the Chair nevertheless is always subject to appeal. There is no ruling or action by the Chair that cannot be appealed, with the rare exception of a ruling based upon a clear and unmistakable reading of the bylaws, which, properly, cannot be appealed.

An appeal is a challenge by a member, which may but need not be seconded, requiring the Chair to put the question to the assembly as to whether a ruling or action by the Chair should be sustained. Someone, for example, might appeal the Chair's ruling on a point of order raised as to whether or not a proposed amendment is relevant to the motion it proposes to amend. If, when the assembly votes on the appeal, the Chair fails to get at least one-half the vote, then the challenger has won the appeal and the Chair must immediately change the ruling or action.

Technically, an appeal is fully debatable. In practice, however, if the issue is clear-cut, the Chair simply puts the question after restating the issue so all know exactly what is being voted on.

When an appeal is made and the Chair is in some doubt as to its merit, the Chair can diplomatically shift the appeal by requesting the assembly to decide the issue. A request by the Chair to the assembly is usually neutral in impact on the Chair, but an appeal can have a negative impact when the assembly does not sustain the Chair's ruling.

When federal, state, or local laws or the organization's own bylaws mandate or prohibit certain actions by the assembly, the assembly cannot appeal a ruling by the Chair that clearly follows them. Vaguely written bylaws may leave some gray areas open to interpretation, but care should be taken that the assembly does not, in effect, attempt to rewrite the bylaws with appeals. In these extreme cases, the Chair should refuse to entertain the appeal, although obviously some diplomacy and reason must be used in such a refusal.

POINTS OF PERSONAL PRIVILEGE

Another way in which members can raise matters on their own initiative is by requesting a point of personal privilege. This item takes precedence in the usual order for recognition, but the exact precedence depends on the purpose of the point.

High Privilege: Procedural Points of Personal Privilege

If a member cannot participate effectively in the meeting for some reason, then the person may raise a point of personal privilege. Examples are situations in which something physical is amiss: the microphone in one area of the hall is dead; the air conditioning is much too cold; additional chairs are needed if all delegates are to be seated. The member informs the Chair of the problem, and the Chair provides the remedy, often by asking one of the staff to take care of the problem.

This type of personal privilege is called a *procedural point* because it relates to the procedures of the meeting. It takes precedence over everything else because every member should by right be able to participate fully in the meeting. Though the meeting should not be forced to come to a halt until the problem is remedied, still the item is of such great importance that the member can interrupt the usual speaking order of debate to be heard.

On the Chair's becoming aware that a member wishes to be recognized in order to make a procedural point of personal privilege, the Chair should stop whatever is happening, even interrupting a speaker who is to continue for more than a few minutes, and recognize the point. Once the problem is addressed, business resumes where it left off.

Included in this category are situations in which a member has been attacked or challenged in some way (such as being accused of committing an immoral or illegal act or of holding an undesirable political viewpoint) either by another member during the meeting or by someone outside the meeting, which is revealed during the meeting. In this case, the member may feel that an immediate response is essential. The Chair should then allow the member to respond to the affront.

Low Privilege: Nonprocedural Points of Personal Privilege

Often in a meeting a member wants to extend thanks to the organization for its support in a certain situation or to recognize a fellow member's outstanding accomplishment that might otherwise go unnoticed. Sometimes a distinguished visitor is in the hall and a member knows the Chair would want to recognize the visitor if the person's presence were known.

This category of points of personal privilege, even though important to an individual member, is not on the agenda and should never be allowed to take over a significant part of a meeting. It is not reasonable to hold members to strict limits on debate, the agenda, and other disciplines of the meeting and then turn over substantial blocks of time for members to speak to nonprocedural points of personal privilege that are not important contributions to the meeting. There is no traditional name for this category, and I shall call them simply nonprocedural points of personal privilege, or points of personal privilege for the good of the organization.

Such points can have to do with a member's personal experience with the organization — the member wants to "point with pride" or "view with alarm" — or with the experience of others. Examples are wide in range. They can include a member's great satisfaction that an association goal has been met or concern over a lack of decorum in assembly meetings. The member may want to inform the assembly of a significant recognition received by the organization through, say, an editorial in the press. The examples in this category are as varied as the members' experiences.

In years past, organizations sometimes provided for this type of statement by specifying a time on the agenda when members could make observations that related to the organization or, in the usual parlance, statements "for the good of the order." The use of the practice and, indeed, the term are no longer popular. But there is almost always some need to allow such individual statements to be made.

My advice is that the organization accept this type of nonprocedural point of personal privilege as a fact of life and work out a method for dealing with it positively. The alternative is that these points may arise throughout the meeting, forcing the Chair to handle them almost defensively. For example, consider a situation in which an assembly has as its next item its budget, which for this meeting is the most critical item of concern to all members. Then someone rises to a nonprocedural point of personal privilege to tell the assembly of the accomplishments of a local unit that put on a successful rummage sale. What can the Chair do? All the members probably want to get on with the budget, but the nonprocedural point can take from three to five minutes. More than likely, the Chair will ask the member to defer this point until after the budget, resulting in a slight chilling effect on the meeting.

The better solution is to have a standing rule adopted by the assembly that (1) clearly gives the Chair discretion over recognition of nonprocedural points of personal privilege and (2) sets out a time at the very end of the meeting for their recognition. In this way, the Chair has control over the orderly flow of the business on the agenda (which, remember, the assembly voted to accept) and the individual still has some opportunity for a nonprocedural point to be heard. Of course, the assembly can always vote to adjourn before all the points are heard at the end of the meeting, but that risk cannot be eliminated.

The NEA does not have a rule to this effect but, by custom, has developed this procedure over the years. At the end of its annual four-day representative assembly, after the delegates have transacted all their business, those who wish to hear these statements of nonprocedural points of personal privilege remain in their seats for about an hour while some thirty to forty points are made. Though the members making these points would no doubt prefer that every seat be filled as they speak, they have the substantial benefit of actually being heard, and their remarks are included in the verbatim transcript of the proceedings. In other words, this procedure is a compromise in which the majority of the eight thousand members is accorded preference, but the individual member is still heard and recorded.

CHAPTER 12

Decisions by the Assembly

*T*he preliminaries (the notice, credentials, rules, and agenda), the motions, and the debate are all critical to the democratic process, but the decisions of the assembly are the ultimate purpose of parliamentary procedure.

The decisions of the assembly, determined by the votes of the members, fall into two categories: a vote on a motion that proposes an action or position to be taken by the organization and a vote in an election in which members choose among candidates for office.

There are many variations on these categories. For example, an assembly can hold an election by simply taking aye and no votes on each candidate, and the candidate who receives a simple majority wins office. Thus, the election is handled in the same way as a regular motion. Conversely, if there are several options before an assembly seeking a solution to a particular problem, the Chair can ask the members to consider them and vote as though the options were opposing candidates for elected office. These variations are as extensive as the mind is creative. The variations, however, always utilize one or both of the two basic categories, so this book focuses only on them.

VOTING ON MOTIONS

Motions, as we saw in Chapter 9 must always be put in the form of a question that allows only one of two responses: aye or no. There can be no in-between position.

Putting the Question

Once all members who desire to speak have been recognized and have spoken, or debate has been closed by the Chair or by vote of the assembly, the Chair puts the question — that is, places the motion before the assembly for a vote.

No member can be forced to vote; even the maker of the motion may abstain. The Chair does not customarily ask for the abstentions to identify themselves. If the number of abstentions is important, however, either as a means of determining a quorum or for measuring the support for an issue, the Chair can ask for the abstentions or a member may make a request that they be counted.

Voting

Voting can be done in several ways, depending on the number of members in the assembly and on the closeness of the vote. These ways were briefly discussed in connection with timing in Chapter 2.

The easiest and quickest vote (other than unanimous consent) is the *voice vote*. The Chair asks that all those who favor the adoption of the motion say aye and all those who oppose the adoption say no. The Chair determines which side prevails. Care should be taken by the Chair when judging the volume of sound because the word *no* is in a lower sound range and will seem louder than the number actually voting. In other words, a hundred noes sound louder than a hundred ayes, in most cases.

When in any doubt, the Chair should ask for a visual count,

or a *division*. In this case, the Chair asks that members either raise a hand or stand in place. This division is not a counted vote but simply a visual estimation of the vote by the Chair. A single member may demand a division by either formally requesting it of the Chair or simply shouting out "Division!" This demand for a division does not require a second and must immediately be honored by the Chair. If there is no demand for a division and the assembly moves on to other business, a member cannot later demand one; it comes too late. But in very large conventions with several thousand delegates, some judgment must be used by the Chair because it may be very difficult for a delegate's shout to be heard, and the system that is being used for recognition may take time. In those cases, it is best to go back for the division, even though there has been some intervening business.

A Chair who is still in doubt after a visual estimation of the vote can ask that the votes be counted. If the members themselves have doubt as to the division vote, they can demand a *counted vote* on a motion to that effect. If the organization has no rule governing this situation, the adoption of this motion requires only a simple majority because it is simply a request of the body. Most organizations, however, have found that it is much wiser, and more expedient in practice, to have a smaller number of the members, usually one-third, empowered by the standing rules to demand a counted vote. One-third is a better fraction because a close vote — for example, 49–51 — will produce the same close vote on the question of taking a counted vote, and the Chair has exactly the same problem as on the vote on the main motion.

Though the vote on the question of a counted vote will not necessarily track exactly as the original close vote — 49–51, in our example — it will in most cases be the same. The reason for this result is that an issue this closely contested normally comes to a vote after heated debate and the positions of the members have become relatively polarized. Remember that in our example the 49–51 split is not known as a fact in the voice vote by either the Chair or the assembly. The Chair has simply estimated the vote by sound alone (a fairly wild guess in this example) and announced which side the Chair thinks prevailed. No one actually knows which side prevailed on a voice vote this close.

Therefore, the polarized group of members who prevailed in the vote estimated by the Chair will all vote against a counted vote — they have nothing to gain and could possibly lose. The group who lost on the estimated vote will all vote for the counted vote because they believe, or at least hope, that the Chair estimated incorrectly in ruling that they had lost. There are dramatic exceptions to this generalized observation. Assume the same example but add the factor that the moral standards of the members might lead to one vote but political reality standards might lead to a different vote. Such an issue might be a question concerning gun control in the state of Utah voted upon in a Democratic convention. The relatively anonymous voice vote and the publicly visible counted vote might vary widely.

In any event, since the usual cause for doubt is a close vote, the Chair should go to a counted vote if there is substantial support for it, regardless of any rule. Otherwise, the doubt will linger throughout the remainder of the meeting.

In small groups, the Chair can take the count or have some other officer such as the secretary do it. In large conventions, it is wise to make preparations for a team of tellers to perform this function. The count is then usually taken within delegations, with the chair of each delegation responsible for an accurate count of that group. But this division of the vote-counting responsibility should not entail the individual delegations' putting the question. To do so will probably end in confusion because of the likelihood that different delegation leaders will ask the question in different forms.

For example, the main motion could be to oppose any burning of the American flag; a delegation leader might restate the question as a test of loyalty to the flag. The only sure way to have every delegate vote on the same question in the same form is to have the assembly Chair put the question. The Chair should ask those who are in favor to stand and remain standing until all those voting aye have been counted within their delegation. Then the assembly Chair should ask those who are opposed to stand and remain standing until they have been counted. In this way, it is certain that everyone will have voted on the same motion.

One technique that tellers can use is to ask that, as each standing delegate within a delegation is counted, that person sit down. That way, there is less chance of confusion as to which members have been counted and which have not. This technique is also helpful to the Chair, who can immediately call for the "opposed" votes when all the "for" votes are seated.

The general practice is to close the hall's doors when the Chair announces that there will be a counted vote. The principle underlying the closed doors is that the counted vote is not an entirely new vote but a more accurate verification of the previous vote, and there should be no changes in the members who voted previously. There is also the consideration that only those members who were present and heard the debate are fully informed, so that it is they who are qualified to participate in the vote. But being fully informed is not the usual threshold qualification in any other vote, so this reasoning is not persuasive.

On the same consistency principle, the doors should be closed during a *roll call vote*. There have been compromises in this practice, especially in the U.S. House of Representatives, where members are given several warning bells and time to return for a roll call vote. In the British House of Commons, the practice has evolved into a compromise under which the doors are closed only after a warning bell and two minutes are allowed for all members to return to the chamber to vote.

There are two purposes for a roll call vote. One is to have the most accurate verification of a vote. The other is to make each member declare his or her position publicly. In the latter case, sometimes a roll call vote is held on an amendment or some other matter less critical than the main motion so that managers of a particular side can get an accurate count of members who are with them and identify which members are not. The opposing members can then be approached in hopes of changing their vote.

Because a roll call vote takes much time, the Chair should be very careful that it is not just a delaying tactic. The number of members required to demand a roll call is a simple majority unless the organization has adopted a standing rule setting a smaller number.

A *majority vote* is always required unless otherwise designated and means more than half the votes cast by those present at the meeting and voting (that is, not abstaining). A two-thirds vote means two-thirds of those present and voting. A majority "of the membership" means more than half of all the members, whether present or not and whether voting or not. The Democratic National Convention is an example of an assembly employing this rule; it requires a majority of all delegates (the membership) for certain motions. This type of majority is also referred to as a "constitutional majority."

DECISIONS BY UNANIMOUS CONSENT

One of the most useful votes for an assembly is the vote by unanimous consent. When the Chair believes that substantially the whole assembly is in support of a matter, it serves little purpose to ask that the entire procedure of motion, second, debate, and vote be followed. The Chair can simply state that "without objection" the matter is adopted or the action taken.

For example, say that after the debate has started on a main motion, it becomes evident that the wording in the motion contains grammatical errors and needs correction. Once the needed corrections are pointed out to the assembly, the Chair can state, "Without objection, those grammatical corrections will be made and the motion will read as corrected. Is there objection?" If no one objects, then there has been unanimous consent, and the assembly has, in fact, voted to make the corrections. If there is objection, even by a single member, then there is not unanimous consent and the usual amendment procedure must be used to make the corrections.

One of the most frequent uses of this motion is to handle a "friendly amendment." For example, the main motion is before the assembly and a floor amendment is proposed. The maker of the main motion approves of the floor amendment and, on proper recognition, announces that he or she will accept the amendment as a friendly amendment. To debate and vote on the issue does not appear necessary, so the Chair asks for unanimous consent in accepting the amendment. (The seconder does not have to agree, only the maker. The maker of the floor amendment and the maker of the main motion fulfill the two-member requirement.)

Unanimous consent, of course, is much stronger than a two-thirds vote. Therefore, a vote on any motion that would otherwise require a two-thirds vote can be taken by unanimous consent. For example, a motion to change the order of business as set out on the agenda already adopted would require a two-thirds vote. If it becomes evident that time problems are developing and the budget should be moved forward in order to have time to consider it fully, the Chair can ask for unanimous consent to do so. Without objection, the item is brought forward.

Similarly, if the body wishes to take some action that is prohibited by the rules, the Chair can suggest to the assembly that, without objection, the rules be suspended and the desired action taken. If there is no objection, the rules are suspended and the action is approved. If there is objection, the Chair must ask for a vote.

More often, unanimous consent is used for a minor issue not requiring the full procedural process for an assembly decision. The Chair might not ask specifically for unanimous consent, but simply announce an intended action — say, to allow a nondelegate to speak when it is clear that all wish to hear this person. Hearing no objection, the Chair proceeds accordingly. The test in these cases is whether the assembly understands exactly what the Chair is proposing. If they do understand and there is no objection, then it can be inferred that consent has been given. (If the meeting is a large one, the Chair may wish to be a little more formal and actually ask if there is objection.)

MOTION TO DIVIDE
THE QUESTION

At any time prior to the vote on a main motion, the assembly may divide the question by a simple majority vote, provided that the main motion contains more than one independent provision. The provisions may be related, but to be divided each must be free-standing so that should one pass and the other fail, the part of the question that passed would still make sense and be a whole proposition.

The report of the resolutions committee is an excellent

example. This report often contains a number of independent resolutions relating to different subjects. Some may be controversial while others are not. The assembly may select those resolutions it wishes to debate and vote on separately while leaving the other noncontroversial resolutions to be adopted en masse.

Motions other than main motions can also be divided as long as they meet the requirement of containing at least two independent provisions. For example, an amendment could contain two paragraphs, both relevant to the main motion but clearly divisible. In that case, the amendment could be divided into two parts before the final vote and the two voted on separately.

Some writers allow a single member to demand a division of the question. A better practice is to put the question for vote of the assembly. The basis for this stricter standard is that most organizations today use a committee system in which much of the consideration and debate on substantive issues takes place in committees. If the committee has done its work well, it is extremely frustrating for only one member to be able to force each item to be fully debated again when the committee makes its report. For example, say a resolutions committee has recommended fifty resolutions after many hours or even days of work and compromise. If one member can force each resolution to be considered again by the full assembly, not only have the committee's efforts been wasted, but the assembly will need more than eight hours in which to handle the report. (Experience teaches that an average of ten minutes is required for a good-sized assembly to consider a single item of substantive business under the usual rules of debate.) The one-member standard for demanding a division of the question simply renders the committee system ineffective. The majority of the assembly can, of course, divide items if it wishes to, but the assembly should not become hostage to one member who may be trying only to disrupt the meeting.

RECONSIDERATION OF A VOTE
PREVIOUSLY TAKEN

After an assembly has voted on a question, that issue, or substantially the same one, cannot be brought back before the assembly a second time during the same session except by means of a motion to reconsider. This motion requires a majority vote if it is made on the same day or the next day after the matter to be reconsidered was voted upon or if notice of this motion has been given. If the motion to reconsider is made later than the next day and notice has not been given, a two-thirds vote is required. If the motion for reconsideration of the vote on that question fails, the motion to reconsider cannot be brought up again during the same session.

Some members use this motion to avoid having a controversial question come up again; they move for reconsideration immediately following the vote on that question. Since the same members are still in place, and the substantive question has just been voted on, the members will almost always vote *not* to reconsider the vote just taken, thus settling the issue for that session.

A member wishing to have a vote reconsidered may inform the Chair at any time, even during debate on another matter. The Chair must receive the notice when it is given but has discretion as to when the motion to reconsider will be debated and voted on so long as it is done before adjournment that day.

Some writers stipulate that to move reconsideration, the maker of this motion must have voted on the prevailing side and have had a change of heart (otherwise, the mover wouldn't want the reconsideration). The basis for this rule is that unless at least one member has changed sides, the motion for reconsideration is dilatory — a waste of the assembly's time. In practice, however, this rule is not effective, and I reject it. In most meetings, any number of members will usually volunteer to change their vote in order to accommodate another member in the spirit of democracy or good sportsmanship. Also, a foresighted member can ask for a standing division after the first vote in which the member's position has been defeated and then change to the prevailing side in the second vote, thus acquiring the right to make the motion for reconsideration. It is more efficient and conducive to honesty to allow any member to make the motion.

Once the motion to reconsider is made, debate follows as for any main motion. Although the specific question is whether or not the original vote should be reconsidered and the assembly should debate that issue once more, the entire substance of the issue can be debated at this point. The merits of the issue are clearly relevant to whether the question should be debated and voted on again.

If the motion to reconsider fails, the issue is settled with finality for that session. If it passes, the assembly returns to consideration and debate of the issue at precisely that point in debate at which the vote to be reconsidered was originally taken. For example, if a main motion has been amended three times and is adopted as amended, there can be a motion later in the meeting to reconsider the specific vote on only the second amendment. If that vote for reconsideration of the second amendment passes, then the assembly returns to the point when the main motion was pending and the first amendment had been adopted but not the second or the third; debate would resume specifically on the question as to the adoption of the second amendment. After the debate and vote on the second amendment, the third amendment might have to be debated and voted upon again if its status was dependent upon the original vote on the second amendment and the reconsideration of the second amendment has resulted in a substantial change.

The sponsor of the motion to reconsider is given preference on recognition, once debate is resumed. Presumably, that member has additional information, a compromise, or a perfecting amendment to offer that will persuade the assembly to reach a different result on the second vote.

A variation of the motion to reconsider is the motion to rescind. This motion traditionally has been used when the time deadline for the motion to reconsider to be made — one legislative day — has passed. In contrast, the motion to rescind has no time limit. There is, however, another, substantial limit on this motion. It can be used only in the case of an affirmative vote; a vote that has failed cannot be rescinded.

In this book, I have changed the traditional motion to reconsider so that it can be brought up at any time; it is thus more useful. Since the motion to reconsider can be applied to either a vote that passed or a vote that failed, use of my changed motion to reconsider avoids the hindering limitations of both traditional motions. For example, say a meeting that has voted down a by-law amendment does not adjourn, but rather adjourns to meet again at the call of the Chair. Several weeks later, the Chair recalls the members, and because of new information or other events, the assembly wishes to change the vote on the bylaw amendment that failed. Under my rule on reconsideration, the assembly can reconsider the negative vote — by a simple majority with notice or a two-thirds vote without notice.

This example illustrates both the greater usefulness of the motion to reconsider and the fact that this motion can require only a simple majority for reconsideration (with notice in this example) even though the adoption of the bylaw amendment would require a two-thirds vote.

NOMINATIONS AND ELECTIONS

The bylaws should set out in some detail the basic provisions for nominations and elections. Candidates can then prepare their campaigns and speeches with some certainty about the process rather than be forced to adapt on the spot to last-minute decisions of the assembly. For example, the bylaws should specify the time limit for acceptance speeches by candidates; in that way, they can prepare their speeches well before the meeting, confident that the limit will not be changed just before they are to speak.

In the event that bylaw or standing rule provisions are lacking, the assembly can decide these matters by simple majority vote at the time, but these decisions should precede the nominating process and not interrupt it.

Nominations

Every member in an assembly can nominate any other eligible member for office unless there is a bylaw provision that restricts this right. Bylaws often require that a nomination petition be signed by a given number of delegates so that the speaking time is not filled with candidates who are not viable. Another bylaw provision might require that a nominated candidate agree in writing to run for office so that time is not taken up with candidates who withdraw later. The bylaws can also set out such standards for holding office as the number of years a member must have belonged to the organization before taking office. And to facilitate the nominating committee's determination of compliance with such standards, the bylaws should require that a written notice of nomination be submitted early enough to give the committee time to perform this task.

Some organizations have a bylaw providing that a candidate must be nominated and that any votes for a candidate not nominated are void. Such a provision ensures that all standards of eligibility to hold office have been met and that the candidate is willing to serve if elected.

Bylaws often provide for a *nominating committee* whose duty it is to present a slate of nominees to the assembly. Although there is no universally accepted practice, sound judgment often requires that the nominating committee be selected by the board of directors or some other governance group, not by the president. Some organizations prohibit the president from even serving on the nominating committee. Practice varies on whether the committee presents one nominee for each office to be filled or more than one. A set of one nomination for each office to be filled is often referred to as a "slate." Sometimes the nominating committee presents a slate, and a faction in the organization presents a competing slate.

After the nominating committee has presented its report, which places the names of its nominees in consideration, the Chair should then call for *nominations from the floor.* Any candidate nominated from the floor must still meet all of the eligibility requirements of the organization. The principle of open nominations, in which every member may nominate any other eligible member, is a basic principle of parliamentary procedure in the United States. Nominations should not be closed until a reasonable time has passed. If a motion to close nominations comes too quickly, the Chair should ask that the motion be deferred until it is certain that there are no further nominations. Some organizations make a practice of calling for further nominations three times before closure, but there is no standard required other than a reasonable time. The Chair can then close nominations, without motion and vote, by stating, "Nominations for the office of treasurer are now closed." Once closed, nominations cannot be reopened for that office, except by a majority vote of the assembly on a request that they be reopened.

Although it is acceptable to have a motion to close nominations come from the floor, such a motion is not needed because the Chair will not put the motion until after all floor nominations have been made. At that point, there is no one resisting closure because everyone wishing to make a nomination has done so. In short, the motion to close nominations cannot be put until there is unanimous consent to close nominations. Once it is apparent to the Chair that there are no further nominations, the Chair might just as well declare nominations closed rather than put the question to a formal vote. If such a motion has been made, however, it is probably more expedient for the Chair to call for a vote.

Elections

The standing rules should contain detailed provisions for the handling of elections. In this way, the organization will have already settled such questions as what to do when there are several candidates for an office and none receives a majority vote: which candidates shall appear on the second (runoff) ballot? As in nominations, all questions not covered in the standing rules can be settled by simple majority vote of the assembly at the time of the election, but it is much better to have these matters settled well in advance, when there is less emotion and personalities are not involved.

A basic principle of parliamentary procedure is that a candidate must receive a *majority vote* — that is, a majority of those present and voting — to be elected. The bylaws or rules can change this standard, but it is not usually advisable and most organizations keep this basic requirement.

There are, however, certain cases in which an organization believes that it is reasonable and expedient to change that standard to a *plurality vote*. The most common instance is one in which there are several positions to be filled, such as membership on a committee, and customarily there are many more candidates than positions. Another common example is in the case of a mailed ballot in which the leadership does not want to incur the expense of a later runoff ballot. Sometimes there is a logistical problem: in a two-day convention, the vote must be scheduled for the second day and there is not enough time to hold a runoff election. In this case, the provision in the standing rules or the decision announced from the Chair (without objection or by vote of the assembly) would be that the candidates will fill the positions in the order of the number of votes they receive.

This same policy can be followed if there are several candidates for positions and more candidates receive a majority than there are positions to be filled. Although a candidate who has received a majority vote will have to be dropped in this situation, it seems fairer to drop the majority-vote candidates who received fewer votes than to put the other majority-vote candidates who were the front-runners at risk on a second ballot. This policy can be debated, but a wiser approach is to provide for this situation, as the organization thinks best, in the standing rules.

The question of dropping names from the ballot can also arise when there are a number of candidates for the *same* office. Too often, when there is no governing standing rule provision, the assembly will not think about this problem until after the first ballot. For example, after first-ballot results are announced, someone moves that, in view of the results, the second ballot should be taken with "only the two candidates who received the most votes" or "with the bottom three candidates dropped from the ballot." Either of these approaches could be an acceptable way of handling the ballot — but only *before* the ballot is taken, *not just after*. Thus, in this case, the proper motions would be (1) that all names continue on the second ballot and (2) that if no candidate receives a majority vote, the top two names should appear on a third ballot (or the bottom three members be dropped). It is critical to have this type of decision made in advance of the ballot. It is not fair to wait to see the results and then determine which names should be dropped.

A bylaw provision requiring a *written ballot* is highly desirable in that this is the most reliable method of taking a count in an election. If questions arise, the ballots, which should always be saved for a reasonable time, can be examined and counted again. The written ballot also protects the member who might be intimidated in an open, public vote. This latter protection is not always desirable, as in the case of the Democratic party, whose charter prohibits secret ballots; each member must take a public stand. Labor unions, on the other hand, are required by federal law to have secret ballots.

In small assemblies, as well as large assemblies in which the custom is simply to elect the slate proposed by the nominating committee, the election can be conducted by means *other than a ballot* — by voice vote, by a division (standing vote or show of hands), or by a counted vote. (See pp. 120–123.) The pitfalls of these methods are obvious, and the nonballot election should be avoided in all cases except those in which one of these methods clearly cannot go wrong for reasons apparent at the time. For example, the Chair may be absolutely certain that one candidate's support is overwhelming and the only opposition is a token candidate. These cases should be carefully judged, however, and the ballot used if there is the smallest doubt.

Finally, in certain circumstances, an election may be by *acclamation,* or unanimous consent — although this is not permissible if there is any objection. Exception: Political conventions customarily call the roll by states until all have had the opportunity to report their vote and the nomination of one candidate is arithmetically certain. At that point, the Chair entertains a motion for nomination by acclamation. Although there is little question that some delegates still privately object to that candidate and there is not actually unanimous consent, the matter is brought to a dramatic and noisy close by this vote.

In other organizations, acclamation is often used when there is only one candidate for the office. If an organization has a bylaw provision requiring a written ballot (which is the recommended procedure), election by acclamation is not possible unless the bylaws also provide for it. The bylaws cannot be suspended, but they can take cognizance of this instance of an uncontested candidate.

However the election is conducted, once it is underway, the Chair should not entertain any motion of any kind that would interrupt the voting, including a motion to adjourn. The Chair can answer only points of order related specifically to the manner in which the election is being handled at that time. Once all members have voted and the tellers have begun their task of counting the votes, the Chair can proceed with other elections or business, unless what is to be considered is dependent on the outcome of the election.

Each assembly should have an *election committee,* also

sometimes called a *tellers committee,* or some appropriate group to count the votes and report the results to the assembly. This report is only the committee's recommendation to the assembly, and it should be moved for adoption, debated if necessary, and voted on. If the report is not adopted for some reason, the committee must return and either conduct a recount and come forward with another report or inform the assembly that it cannot resolve the problem and there must be another election.

The basic principle here is that the assembly itself not only determines how elections are to be conducted (those areas not already provided for in the bylaws or standing rules) but also controls and makes the final judgment on the results of an election. If there is a question of misunderstanding or of fraud, the assembly should not adopt the committee's report but take whatever action it judges to be appropriate. It can vote to hold a new election replacing the challenged one or send the election committee back with instructions to recount or reexamine the ballots and make another report.

Once the election committee report is adopted, the assembly has given its approval to the entire nomination and election process. The election is over. Although a later motion to reconsider the vote on the report is permissible, such a motion should be entertained by the Chair only in cases in which new information could change the outcome of the election (information not available at the time the report was adopted) or in clear cases of fraud. Clerical or minor errors that are not outcome-determinative should be noted but should not be the basis for a new election.

CHAPTER 13

Recording and Adjournment

Two housekeeping items are the minutes and adjournment. Members do not usually pay much attention to either, but both can be critical in certain situations.

THE MINUTES

It is important to keep an accurate record of all actions taken by any assembly. Some organizations also want to keep a record of the debate relating to the actions taken, even to the extent of having a verbatim transcript of the entire proceedings. The degree of detail to be recorded on debate is flexible, but all actions — that is, motions adopted or rejected — should be included in the record.

The reasons for this accurate record are obvious, especially with organizations that may face later legal challenges to some action in the meeting. As I've indicated, courts of law do not eagerly intervene in the actions of private (as opposed to public) organizations. But if there is a clear showing that the basic principles of due process (notice, fairness) were not followed or if there was outright fraud, then the courts could become involved. An accurate record in the minutes is the best evidence in such situations.

Even if there is no legal challenge, the members of the organization need to have some assurance that their actions in the meeting are not forgotten and that there is accountability. The secretary of the organization is responsible for preparing a draft set of minutes — regardless of their detail — and submitting them for approval at the next meeting of the organization. They may be read at the meeting but in fact seldom are, especially if they are printed and distributed beforehand.

On a motion, the members are asked to verify the accuracy of the minutes, either as read or as printed and distributed. If they were distributed, it is not necessary to include in the motion a provision that the reading be dispensed with.

Errors in the minutes may be corrected by amendment in the usual way of handling amendments. Obvious minor errors, such as misspellings, can be corrected by unanimous consent.

No action already taken can be changed by changing the minutes. Think of the minutes as a report on the weather at the last meeting: you cannot change what the weather did on that day. Nor can you change what the members did; you can correct only a misstatement as to what actually happened.

ADJOURNMENT

The members of an assembly are never prisoners of the meeting but can vote to terminate it at any time, even while a motion is pending and in full debate. The one exception to this rule is that the motion to adjourn (or to recess) is not in order while the assembly is actually voting. With this one exception, the motion to adjourn takes precedence over all other matters.

A *recess* is a short adjournment; the only difference is the length of time for which the meeting is adjourned. For example, to adjourn for one hour for lunch is customarily referred to as a recess. The procedure, however, is the same.

The motion to adjourn cannot be debated, and the Chair should put it to an immediate vote. There are some exceptions, however. If the motion is made with some additional language — for example, as to length of time for the adjournment or as to a date when the assembly should again meet — then the motion would be debatable and amendable as to the time or the date.

Another variation of the simple motion to adjourn is the motion to adjourn the meeting until a specified later time. This is an extraordinary motion and should be used only with care. It provides for a continuation of the *same* meeting to start again at the point at which the motion to adjourn was adopted — with the same members, the same rules, and the same agenda. Since the notice requirements have already been met for that meeting, new notice is not legally required. Good judgment and fair play, however, advise new notice for the continuation of the adjourned meeting if it is at all possible. A typical example of the use of this motion is the situation in which the assembly cannot possibly complete all its business in the time allocated and must continue a few days later. But that does not allow time for the group to meet the legal requirements for a published notice for a new meeting, so the assembly adjourns the present meeting to a specified later time, which obviates the need for notice.

There is a variation of this kind of adjournment: the meeting adjourned until it is reconvened at the call of the Chair. This variation entails some risk because there is no announced time, and there can be considerable controversy if the Chair decides, for example, to call the meeting back into session on the Fourth of July. There are some extreme cases in which this motion could be useful, but great care should be taken to give advance notice for reconvening the assembly.

MODEL STANDING RULES AND BYLAWS

Model Standing Rules

*T*he following model set of standing rules includes substantially all the essential rules for any meeting; some items have been left blank where the rule depends on choices made by an individual organization. Even where there are no blanks, some changes may be necessary in order for these rules to meet the needs of a particular organization.

Although bylaws are superior in authority to standing rules, I discuss standing rules first because they relate to procedure for meetings, which is more pertinent to our concerns. Bylaws relate to the organization of an association.

STANDING RULES

1. Notice. The President shall prepare or cause to be prepared the notice of a meeting, along with a proposed agenda and all those items that are received by the President for inclusion in the agenda fifteen days prior to the date of meeting. This notice

and the proposed agenda shall then be mailed to all members ten days prior to the meeting.

2. The Chair. The President shall preside at all meetings, serving as the Chair. In the absence of the President, the Vice President shall preside. In the absence of both the President and the Vice President, the order of succession to the duty of presiding shall be the Secretary, the Treasurer, and a member of the Board of Directors.

Once the hour has arrived for which the notice of the meeting was given and the Chair has determined that a quorum is present, then the Chair shall call the meeting to order.

3. Quorum. A quorum for a meeting shall be as provided in the bylaws. As provided in the bylaws, proxies are not permitted for either the establishment of a quorum or for the conduct of business. A quorum must be present for the meeting to be called to order, and a quorum must continue to be present at all times during the meeting. If the Chair observes that a quorum no longer exists, or determines, upon a point of order by a member, that there is no quorum, then no further business shall be conducted other than to recess while efforts are made to obtain a quorum or to adjourn.

4. Agenda. Members who wish to introduce any item of substantive business (other than floor amendments to main motions introduced by committees or other members) shall request that a copy of such substantive business be included in the proposed agenda mailed to all members. Such items received by the President fifteen days prior to the meeting shall be included in the proposed agenda. A member may also give similar notice of that member's proposed floor amendment if these proposed floor amendments are received prior to this same fifteen-day period. If the President believes that an item is out of order, and the matter cannot be reconciled before the notice is mailed to members, the item shall be included, but the President may add a notation that the Chair intends to rule the item out of order.

At the beginning of the meeting, after the reports of the credentials committee and the rules committee, if any, the proposed agenda shall be submitted for adoption, and then additional substantive items may be added or deleted by means of amendment. Once the agenda has been adopted, it cannot be changed except by a two-thirds vote for such change.

Points of personal privilege that do not relate to the ability of members to participate fully in the meeting do not have to be placed on the agenda; the Chair, however, has discretion in requiring previous written notice as to such points of personal privilege and as to the time on the agenda for the recognition of these points. (See Rule 20, below.)

5. Credentials Committee Report. The first item of business of the meeting shall be the adoption of the report of the credentials committee. Any challenge to this report shall be in the form of a floor amendment, adding, deleting, or substituting names on the report. If this report is not ready for adoption at the beginning of the meeting, it shall be presented as soon as practicable thereafter.

6. Rules. These standing rules shall govern the meeting. If a member wishes to amend these rules, notice may be given the President, who shall include any proposed rules amendment in the proposed agenda mailed to all members. With this notice, a rule may be changed by a simple majority vote. Without such notice, these rules may be amended, or suspended for a single meeting, by a two-thirds vote.

The rules committee may propose changes at any meeting by giving notice, with the notice of the meeting mailed to all members, and including such changes in a rules committee report after the credentials committee report.

7. Enforcement of Rules and Appeal. The Chair shall enforce the rules, but a member may appeal a ruling of the Chair. Following a brief statement by the challenging member, and a response by the Chair, the Chair shall put the question, and a simple majority vote (or tie) shall uphold the ruling of the Chair. The Chair may vote on an appeal.

8. Minutes. The Secretary shall maintain a draft set of minutes, which shall be mailed to each member within ten days after the meeting. At the next meeting, these minutes shall be presented for adoption. The minutes may be amended in order to make actual corrections concerning debates or votes, but the minutes cannot be changed in an effort to modify actions previously taken.

9. Motions. All decisions of the meeting are to be made by means of a motion made by a member, seconded by another member (or a committee), stated by the Chair, offered for debate,

and then put to a vote by the Chair. The motion that initiates a new and independent idea or proposal is the main motion. Motions shall be stated in the positive, not in the negative.

10. Debate. The Chair shall give preference to the maker of the motion to speak first, but not to the seconder next. Recognition shall alternate, so far as practicable, between those favoring the question and those opposing the question. No member shall speak for more than _____ minutes during debate, nor speak a second time until all those wishing to speak on that same side of the question have spoken, nor speak a third time in debate. A member may yield that member's remaining time to a second member, but that second member may not then yield to another third member. All debate shall be directed through the Chair, including questions over which the Chair shall exercise control so as to avoid purely rhetorical or argumentative questions.

11. Closing Debate. If the Chair determines that there has been ample debate, with full opportunity for both sides to be heard, or if the Chair sees that, after several speakers, there are no members coming forward in opposition, the Chair, on its own initiative, may propose that debate be closed. If there is objection from the assembly, then the Chair shall proceed to put the question of whether or not to close debate. Any member, upon proper recognition and not taking precedence in any speaking order and without interrupting any other speaker, may move that debate be closed, provided that there has actually been debate on the issue. The motion to close debate is not debatable and requires a two-thirds vote.

12. Amendments. Changes in the main motion may be proposed by means of amendments which:

(a) add to the motion,
(b) delete from the motion, or
(c) delete from the motion and add (or substitute) in the place of the deletion.

Amendments must be relevant. An amendment may be hostile, but it cannot simply negate the motion it seeks to amend, as by adding the word *not* to the proposal. All amendments shall be in writing, with a copy provided to the Chair.

13. Other Dispositions of Main Motions. At any time during

debate of the main motion, a member, upon proper recognition and not taking precedence in any speaking order and without interrupting any other speaker, may move:

(a) to postpone the main motion to some other reasonable time. This motion is debatable and amendable; or

(b) to refer the main motion to a committee or some other group or person. This motion is debatable and amendable.

Upon such motion, the mover shall first be recognized to speak, and then the mover of the main motion shall have preference in recognition to respond. If an amendment to the main motion is pending at the time, then the amendment or amendments shall remain with the main motion if it is postponed or referred.

14. Requests to the Assembly.

(a) Withdrawal of Motions. Once a motion has been stated by the Chair (or distributed to all members in the notice of meeting), it cannot be withdrawn, except upon the approval of the assembly. The maker may request withdrawal, and if there is no objection, it shall be withdrawn. If there is objection, then withdrawal shall require a simple majority vote.

(b) Divide the Question. If the pending motion contains two or more independent matters, the assembly may divide the motion for debate and the vote (or just for the vote) by a majority vote.

(c) Other Requests. Any other request that does not require a suspension of the rules may be approved by a majority vote.

15. Voting. The Chair shall put the question and ask for the "ayes" and "noes" by voice vote. If the Chair is in doubt, or upon the request of a single member (who may simply shout "Division!" without being recognized), the Chair shall make a visual estimate of the vote, either by a show of hands or by a standing vote. If the Chair is still in doubt, the Chair may request that the vote be counted. Upon a motion by a member, the assembly may require a counted vote by a one-third standing vote for such count.

A roll call vote, in which each individual member's vote is

recorded, or a vote by written ballot may be required upon a simple majority vote of the assembly.

16. Reconsidering a Vote Previously Taken. A member may request a reconsideration of any vote taken earlier that same day or the previous legislative day (i.e., the previous day excluding weekend days and holidays on which meetings were not held). This motion is debatable. If a member wishes to reconsider a previous vote later than the next legislative day, actual notice must be given either by at least one day's oral notice to the assembly while it is in session or by written notice to be included in the notice of the meeting sent to all members. Without such notice, a two-thirds vote is required in order to reconsider a previous vote later than the next legislative day.

If the motion for reconsideration passes, the assembly shall return to the point in debate at which the reconsidered vote was taken. The sponsor of the motion to reconsider shall be the first speaker recognized, and debate shall proceed as though the reconsidered vote had never been taken.

17. Adjournment. The motion to adjourn is in order at any time, except during a vote, and is not debatable unless there is included in the motion a time to adjourn or a time to reconvene the meeting. A short adjournment, such as several minutes or the time necessary for lunch, may be referred to as a "recess."

18. Committees and Committee Reports. When a standing or a special (ad hoc) committee presents a report to the assembly, the report shall not last more than ten minutes, after which time the chair of the committee shall move the adoption of recommendations, if any, contained in the report. If the committee report contains no recommendations for adoption, then the chair of the committee shall conclude the report by stating that the report is being filed for information and that no vote is necessary. The motion to adopt the committee's report need not be seconded as it has the majority support of the committee (more than one member). Minority reports may be submitted as proposed amendments to the committee's report. The minority members shall propose their amendments from the floor, rather than from the podium, as with any other floor amendment.

19. Nominations and Elections. Election to office or to membership on the Board of Directors shall be by written ballot, upon nomination by a member at a meeting for which proper notice

of nominations and elections has been given. There shall be one nominating speech of no more than_____minutes for each candidate and one acceptance speech of no more than_____minutes by each candidate. Only members whose names have been put in nomination and who have either accepted the nomination in person or in writing and who are otherwise qualified to hold the office for which they seek election may be voted upon. A majority vote shall be required for election. If no candidate has received a majority vote, runoff elections shall be held in accordance with procedures announced by the election committee to the assembly before the first election takes place. If no such procedures are announced, then the runoff election shall be held, and the runoff ballot shall list those unsuccessful candidates who, arranged in decreasing order of votes received, equal one more than the number of positions to be filled. If more candidates receive a majority than there are positions to be filled, then the majority vote candidates receiving the most votes, in that order, shall be elected.

20. Points of Personal Privilege. There shall be two categories of points of personal privilege:

(a) Procedural Personal Privilege. If a member's ability to participate fully and effectively in the meeting is hindered in some way, that member has the right to be recognized immediately upon a point of procedural personal privilege, and the Chair shall address the problem. Included in this category are situations in which a member has been attacked or challenged and the member, in good faith, believes that an immediate response is necessary in order to preserve the member's status in the organization.

(b) Nonprocedural Points of Personal Privilege. All other points of personal privilege shall be recognized at the discretion of the Chair. The Chair has the discretion to require that the Chair be provided with written notice of a member's desire to make a point of personal privilege that is not procedural. This notice can be a short summary of the point to be made. The Chair shall defer to the time immediately prior to adjournment all such points that do not, in the Chair's judgment, warrant earlier attention.

Model Bylaws

BYLAWS

Article I   Name

The name of this association shall be_____

_____

(the "Association"), with its headquarters located in

_____, _____.

Article II   Purposes

The purposes of this Association shall be_____

_____

_____.

Article III   Membership

1. The active membership of this Association shall be limited to those persons who_____

_____

_____.

2. Any person who endorses the purposes of the Association may be eligible for associate membership, but associate members may not vote or hold elected office.

3. The dues of active members shall be $_____per year, and the dues for associate members shall be $_____per year.

4. Any member who has not paid dues after sixty days' written notice from the Treasurer shall be terminated as a member; however, a member so terminated may be reinstated upon procedures adopted by the Board of Directors.

5. The membership year and the fiscal year of the Association shall be from _____ [date] through _____ [date].

Article IV   Assembly Meetings

1. The active members shall meet in assembly_____times each year at a place and time selected by the Board of Directors. Special meetings may be called by the President or by a majority vote of the Board of Directors. Only those matters contained in the notice for such special meeting may be acted upon at that special meeting. At least_____days' written notice shall be mailed to all members for all meetings.

2. The Assembly shall have the following powers and duties:
   a. to adopt and amend standing rules and these bylaws;
   b. to adopt an annual budget, prepared by the President and the Treasurer and approved by the Board of Directors;
   c. to elect officers and members of the Board of Directors, with open nominations and a secret ballot.
   d. to adopt statements of policy and take actions appropriate to the purposes of this Association;
   e. to establish special committees that have been recommended for approval by the Board of Directors; and
   f. to act as the final authority on all matters arising in this Association, for which authority has not been given to some other officer or governance body by these bylaws.

3. The quorum at a meeting of the Association shall be_____[a number or a percentage of the membership of the Association]. Proxies are not allowed for either the establishment of a quorum or for the transaction of the business of the Association.

4. The annual meeting of the Assembly shall be at a time and place fixed by the Board of Directors. The agenda for the

annual meeting shall include the election of the officers of the Association and the adoption of the annual budget.

Article V   Officers

1. The officers of the Association shall be a President, a Vice President, a Secretary, and a Treasurer.

2. To be eligible for election to an office of the Association, a member must have been an active member for at least _____ years prior to the date of election and must have agreed to be a candidate for the office.

3. The terms of the officers shall be one year. The term shall begin upon the election of the officer and shall end upon the election of the officer's successor. An officer shall not serve more than three successive full terms. The officers shall receive no compensation for their holding office but shall be reimbursed for the ordinary and necessary expenses incurred in the fulfillment of their Association duties.

4. The powers and duties of the officers shall be as follows:

a. President

   The President shall be the principal representative and spokesperson for the Association; preside at all meetings of the Assembly and the Board of Directors; prepare the proposed annual budget, with the advice of the Treasurer, for submission to the Board of Directors for its approval; supervise the activities of the Association staff within guidelines approved by the Board of Directors; receive notice of any substantive business proposed by members for meetings and prepare and cause the proper notice of all meetings to be sent to the members for such meetings; and otherwise carry out duties customarily associated with the office of President.

b. Vice President

   The Vice President shall assist the President in the duties of that office, as requested by the President, and preside at meetings of the Assembly and the Board of Directors in the absence of the President.

c. Secretary

   The Secretary shall keep an accurate record of the meetings of the Assembly and the Board of Directors and shall prepare and submit minutes for approval. The Secretary shall be the custodian of all offical records and files of the Association.

d. Treasurer

The Treasurer shall cause an accurate set of accounts to be maintained for the Association and shall, with the President, prepare a proposed annual budget. The Treasurer shall have an independent CPA firm conduct an annual audit, which shall then be presented to the Board of Directors for approval.

Article VI   Board of Directors

1. The Board of Directors shall be composed of the officers of the Association and _____ additional members elected for staggered three-year terms at the annual meeting of the Assembly.

2. To be eligible for election to the Board of Directors of the Association, a member must have been an active member of the Association for at least _____ years prior to the date of election and must have agreed to be a candidate to the Board.

3. The Board shall meet at least quarterly and also meet in conjunction with the annual meeting of the Assembly. _____ members shall constitute a quorum.

4. The powers and duties of the Board shall be as follows:

a. to act for the Assembly between meetings of the Assembly;

b. to consider the annual budget, submitted by the President, and, after approving it, submit it to the Assembly for final adoption at the annual meeting;

c. to consider guidelines for Association staff submitted by the President and to approve guidelines to be used by the President in the supervision of this staff;

d. to fix the time and place of the annual meeting and other meetings of the Assembly; and

e. to carry out such other duties and responsibilities as are customarily associated with a Board of Directors.

Article VII Committees

1. There shall be five standing committees of the Association:
   a. Budget and Finance
   b. Elections
   c. Credentials
   d. Bylaws and Rules
   e. Resolutions

Each of the standing committees shall have _____ members serving for staggered three-year terms. The Assembly may approve such other special committees as are submitted to the Assembly for approval by the Board.

2. The President shall appoint all members of committees, with the advice and consent of the Board, and shall serve ex officio on all committees. (Note: If a nominating committee is created, it should be selected by the Board, not by the President.)

Article VIII Authority

1. This Association shall be governed by these bylaws and the standing rules of the Association.

2. The latest edition of *Cannon's Concise Guide to Rules of Order* shall be the parliamentary authority for the Association on matters not governed by the bylaws and the standing rules.

Article IX Amendments
to Bylaws

1. Proposed amendments to these bylaws may be submitted by the Bylaws and Rules Committee, by the Board of Directors, or by written petition signed by _____ active members.

2. Proposed bylaw amendments shall be received by the Bylaws and Rules Committee at least sixty days prior to the meeting at which they are to be considered. The Bylaws and Rules Committee shall make editorial changes as needed and shall contact the sponsor if substantive changes are necessary for the proposed amendment to be in proper order. The Bylaws and Rules

Committee shall cause copies of its final draft of the proposed amendment to be mailed to every member thirty days prior to such meeting. At the meeting, the proposed amendment shall be presented by the chair of the Bylaws and Rules Committee, with either the committee's recommendation for approval or rejection or no position.

3. A two-thirds vote of the members present and voting at the meeting shall be required for adoption of the proposed amendment.

4. Unless otherwise provided for, the amendment shall take effect immediately upon adoption.

Selected Bibliography

BRITISH MANUALS OF PARLIAMENTARY PROCEDURE

Citrine, Walter McLennan. *ABC of Chairmanship*. 4th ed. Revised and edited by Michael Cannell and Norman Citrine. London: NCLC Publishing Society, 1982. 118 pp.

Ilbert, Courtney Palgrave. *Manual of Procedure of the House of Commons*. London: J. B. Nichols, 1984. 222 pp.

Jennings, Ivor. *Parliament*. 2d ed. Cambridge: Cambridge University Press, 1957. 548 pp.

May, Thomas Erskine. *Parliamentary Practice*. 21st ed. Edited by C. I. Boulton, Clerk of the House of Commons. London: Butterworth, 1989. 1,023 pp.

Palgrave, Reginald F. D. *Chairman's Handbook*. 26th ed. London: J. M. Dent, 1964. 104 pp.

Redlich, Josef. *The Practice of the House of Commons*. 3 vols. London: Archibald Constable Co., 1903. 699 pp.

Silk, Paul. *How Parliament Works*. 2d ed. London: Longman Group, 1989. 263 pp.

Smith, James Walter. *Handy Book on the Law and Practice of Public Meetings*. London: Effingham Wilson, Royal Exchange, 1873. 89 pp.

AMERICAN MANUALS OF PARLIAMENTARY PROCEDURE

Cushing, Luther S. *Manual of Parliamentary Practice: Rules for Proceeding and Debate in Deliberative Assemblies*. Philadelphia: David McKay, 1925. 318 pp.

Demeter, George. *Demeter's Manual of Parliamentary Law and Procedures*. Boston: Little, Brown, 1969. 374 pp.

Jefferson, Thomas. *Jefferson's Manual*. Washington: U.S. Government Printing Office, 1988. 194 pp.

Keesey, Ray E. *Modern Parliamentary Procedure*. Boston: Houghton Mifflin, 1974. 175 pp.

Mason, Paul. *Mason's Manual of Legislative Procedure*. St. Paul: West Publishing, 1989. 677 pp.

Oleck, Howard L., and Cami Green. *Parliamentary Law and Practice for Nonprofit Organizations*. 2nd ed. Philadelphia: American Law Institute; American Bar Association: 1991. 160 pp.

Riddick, Floyd M., and Miriam H. Butcher. *Riddick's Rules of Procedure*. Lanham, MD: Madison Books, 1985. 224 pp.

Robert, Henry M. *Robert's Rules of Order Newly Revised*. 9th ed. Glenview, Ill.: Scott, Foresman, 1990. 706 pp.

Sturgis, Alice. *Sturgis Standard Code of Parliamentary Procedure*. 3d ed. New York: McGraw-Hill, 1988. 275 pp.

Glossary

Absentee Member of an organization who is not present at a meeting.

Abstain, abstention The refusal or declining of a member to vote when a vote is being taken. Because an abstention is not a vote, it need not be announced unless there is a special reason for noting the number of abstentions.

Accept *See* **Adopt.**

Acclamation Unanimous consent by the assembly for the election of a candidate. Acclamation suspends all rules.

Action Any activity on the part of the assembly that either decides an issue (such as a vote to adopt the main motion) or postpones or refers the main motion.

Adhere Attach to; for example, an amendment adheres to the main motion it seeks to amend.

Ad hoc The designation for a special committee that describes it as temporary as opposed to standing.

Adjourn   To end a meeting, usually until the next designated time. A short adjournment, such as one hour, is usually referred to as a recess which does not end the meeting.

Adopt   The decision by an assembly to make a motion effective or to put it into effect. Interchangeable with the term *adopt* are the terms *accept, agree to,* and *approve* when those terms describe main motions put to an assembly for a vote.

Agenda   The list of items of business that are to come before the members at a meeting. Prior to its adoption, the list is referred to as the *proposed agenda.* After it is adopted, it is the *final agenda* as adopted. After its adoption no other business may come before the meeting except by a two-thirds vote.

Agree to   *See* **Adopt.**

Amend   To propose a change, called an *amendment,* to the pending motion by means of addition or deletion, or by a combination of deletion and an addition in lieu of the deleted material. This combination is also called a substitute amendment, a substitute motion, or a substitution. *See also* **Substitution.**

Appeal   A challenge by a member to the Chair's ruling concerning parliamentary procedure or any matter that has impact upon the rights of the member or upon the process of the meeting. The Chair may change the ruling after hearing the member's appeal, or the Chair may put the matter to a vote of the assembly.

Approve   *See* **Adopt.**

Assembly   The highest ranking governance body of an organization composed of all the members. *See also* **Delegate, delegate assembly.**

Aye   An affirmative voice vote meaning yes.

Ballot   A procedure for voting on slips of paper or a voting machine by which the vote is secret. Sometimes referred to as a *secret ballot.*

Board of directors   A governance body of an organization. The group's bylaws specify how its members are to be selected and what their duties and powers shall be. This body usually handles administrative matters, whereas the assembly of all members (or the assembly of delegates representing all members) has legislative duties.

Business A matter or item brought before a meeting for a decision by the members by means of a motion. Business can be in the form of a statement of policy, usually called a resolution, a directive for taking action, or a procedural motion related to the other motions.

Bylaws The basic governance document of an organization, which states the agreement among the members as to purpose, qualifications for membership, dues and finances, and other matters of governance.

Call of a meeting The official announcement or notice to all members, usually in writing, that a meeting is to be held. It includes the time, place, and purpose of the meeting.

Call (the meeting) to order The Chair's announcement to the assembly that the meeting is beginning, thus ruling that a quorum is present and that it is appropriate for the business of the meeting to commence. *See also* **Convene.**

Call the roll A method of taking a vote in which each member's name is called out and each member's vote is announced publicly by that member. This method can also be used to determine attendance of members. *See also* **Vote.**

Chair The person who presides over or conducts the business of a deliberative body. The use of the term *chairman* is no longer recommended; it should be used to designate males only, and *chairwoman* should be used to designate females. Although *chairperson* is acceptable, *chair* is preferred.

Close debate The termination of debate of the question before the assembly, either by an announcement from the Chair (when appropriate, as when no further speakers seek to be recognized for debate) or by two-thirds vote of the undebatable motion to close debate made by a member from the floor. This represents the decision to vote immediately on the pending motion.

Committee A body composed of members selected or elected to perform specific tasks for the organization and to report back to the assembly. A board of directors can also have committees composed of board members who report to the board. *See also* **Special committee; Standing committee.**

Consensus   The state of mutual agreement among members as to the decision on a matter without a vote. To reach a consensus, an assembly usually must allow extensive discussion without limits until all views have been expressed and a common course of action or position has evolved.

Consideration   *See* **Debate.**

Constitution   When the bylaws of an organization are divided into two governance documents, the document that is the more difficult to amend is considered the superior authority and is called the constitution. The other document is called the bylaws. Many organizations today have only a single document referred to as bylaws.

Convene   To call an assembly to order, thus initiating the meeting.

Convention   An assembly of delegates elected to represent groupings of members, such as a district or a state. *See also* **Assembly; Delegate, delegate assembly.**

Counted vote   A vote in which members standing or raising their hands for or against a proposal are actually counted rather than their numbers being estimated.

Credentials committee   The committee which has the duty to determine how many and which members (or delegates, and sometimes also alternates, in the case of a delegate assembly) are entitled to attend and vote at the meeting.

Debate   The formal statements for and against a matter brought before the assembly following the rules of parliamentary procedure. Also called *deliberation* or *consideration*.

Delegate, delegate assembly   A member representing other members according to some formula, such as one delegate for each hundred members in a district or state. Their meeting is called a delegate assembly.

Deliberation   *See* **Debate.**

Dilatory   Describes any inappropriate statement or procedure by a member that delays the progress of business.

Discussion   Debate or consideration of the matter before the assembly.

Division, in voting   A standing vote or a show of hands that may be demanded by a single member or ordered on the initiative of the Chair, which is then estimated visually by the Chair.

Division of the question   When a question before an assembly contains two or more matters that could stand alone if divided into independent questions for the assembly to decide, the question may be divided.

Due process   Procedure that is fair in substance and practice.

En bloc   Meaning "as a group," this refers to a series of items being acted on as a whole. For example, a resolution report containing twenty-five separate items may be adopted by one vote or en bloc by an assembly. *See also* **Division of the question.**

Executive director   The chief executive staff officer of an organization; sometimes referred to as the *executive secretary.*

Executive session   A meeting of an assembly in which no one is allowed to attend except members. On occasion certain staff may be present but only when specifically invited by the assembly. Minutes are kept but are restricted in keeping with the degree of secrecy intended for the executive session. (Many states have sunshine laws that prohibit executive sessions by public bodies except in matters involving personnel, litigation, or the purchase of real property.)

Ex officio   By reason of office. For example, the vice president of an organization may automatically serve as a member of a certain committee ex officio rather than by selection or election. An ex officio member has all the rights and duties of any other member, such as the right to debate or to make motions, unless otherwise provided in the governance documents.

Final agenda   *See* **Agenda.**

Floor   A term in parliamentary procedure relating to recognition by the Chair of the member who has the right to speak, as in, "Mr. Jones, having been recognized by the Chair, now has the floor." This term is also used to designate the area where the members are seated facing the Chair during a meeting.

Floor amendment   An amendment which is proposed by a member from the floor during the meeting, as opposed to a committee's amendment proposed from the podium when the committee makes its report.

Floor, to have   When a member of an assembly has been recognized by the Chair, this member is considered to "have the floor" to the exclusion of all other members. This term is also used to describe the status of a motion. When the Chair has stated the motion, it is considered to be the matter "on the floor" before the assembly.

Friendly amendment   An amendment proposed by a member who believes that the proposed amendment would enhance, or at least not harm, the pending motion; the member asks the Chair to request the maker of the pending motion to accept the proposed amendment as a friendly amendment. If the maker accepts the amendment, the Chair then asks the assembly whether it will, without objection, accept the amendment (without debate and formal vote). If the maker or the assembly refuses to accept the proposed amendment without objection, then the proposed amendment must be moved, debated, and voted on as any other floor amendment.

General consent   *See* **Unanimous consent.**

Germane   Describes something, such as an amendment, that is relevant to the matter before the assembly.

Governance documents   The several (usually two or three) basic, written governance documents of an organization, approved by the members as the continuing agreements among themselves concerning their organization's purpose, its requirements for membership, its finances, and the way in which its programs and meetings will be conducted or governed. Because they continue for the life of the organization, with some formality required for amendment (such as notice and a two-thirds vote), these documents provide continuity for the organization. They generally contain only the essential provisions needed and are therefore considered to be the basic governance documents. *See also* **Constitution; Bylaws; and Standing Rules.**

Hostile Describes something, such as an amendment, that is contrary or opposed to the purpose of the main motion. As long as a hostile motion is relevant, however, it is in order.

House A term in parliamentary procedure meaning the same as *assembly*. *House,* in the British Parliament, designates the House of Commons, and in the U.S. Congress, the House of Representatives.

Illegal vote A vote, usually on a ballot, that cannot be counted because it is unintelligible, is cast for a noneligible candidate, or otherwise violates the rules concerning that vote. An illegal vote cast by a member entitled to vote is nevertheless included in the computation of the total number of votes cast for purposes of determining a majority.

In order Parliamentarily correct and appropriate at a particular time.

Main motion *See* **Motion.**

Majority vote More than half of the votes cast. If, for example, 15 votes are cast, $7\frac{1}{2}$ is half and a majority is 8. If 16 votes are cast, 8 is half and a majority is 9. Also referred to as a simple majority as opposed to a two-thirds majority, a 75 percent majority, or some other majority.

Meeting An official assembly of the members of an organization in one area to conduct the business stated in the call of the meeting. This assembly continues without interruption, except for short breaks or recesses, until an adjournment ends the meeting.

Minority report The report from a body of members, usually a committee, reflecting the position of a minority of its members on an issue, as distinct from the position of the majority which approved the body's report as made to the assembly. Sometimes an organization's rules will provide requirements (such as 25 percent of the committee membership in support) for a minority report to be included in the written report of the committee and presented from the podium; otherwise, there is no special status for a minority report, and the members in the minority must speak and propose amendments from the floor.

Minutes   The written record of the deliberations and decisions of an assembly. Minutes are usually prepared by the secretary and approved by a formal vote of the assembly at the next meeting.

Motion   A proposal made for the purpose of obtaining a decision by the members of an assembly. A new, independent proposal put before the assembly for the first time is a substantive motion and is called a *main motion*. A motion affecting the procedure of a meeting is called a *procedural motion*.

Move   To state a motion.

Nomination   A proposal by one member that another eligible member be a candidate for office.

Notice   The announcement to members in advance that certain matters will be proposed at a meeting. Notice may be verbal, as in the case of a member's statement during one meeting concerning an item to be introduced at the next meeting, or in writing, as in the case of items of business included in the written call mailed to all members prior to the meeting.

Objection   A declaration by a member indicating opposition to a matter or a procedure.

Officer   An elected or appointed leader of an organization.

Open nominations   Nomination procedure by which every eligible member has the opportunity to nominate any other member who is eligible and qualified to hold the elective position.

Order of business   *See* **Agenda.**

Organization   A group of individuals who have voluntarily joined together in an organized way and have agreed, through governance documents, how they will pursue their common purpose and govern their affairs.

Out of order   Not parliamentarily correct.

Parliamentarian   A person who advises the Chair on matters concerning parliamentary procedure.

Parliamentary authority   The book specified in an organization's bylaws as the final authority on all questions of parliamentary procedure not otherwise covered in the organization's standing rules or bylaws.

Parliamentary inquiry   A question by a member to the Chair concerning the parliamentary procedure relating to that meeting (as opposed to hypothetical questions, which are not in order).

Pending question   The immediate motion or question before an assembly.

Plurality vote   A vote in which the candidate or proposition that receives the most votes prevails, whether or not it constitutes a majority.

Point of information   A question by a member to the Chair or to the maker of a motion concerning the pending business.

Point of order   The questioning by a member of any matter then before an assembly as to whether the matter is in order. A point of order normally requires a ruling by the Chair.

Point of personal privilege   A matter initiated by a member from the floor, which will be one of two types: (1) a procedural point (that is, a matter that interferes with that member's ability or status to participate effectively in the meeting), which must be addressed immediately; or (2) a non-procedural point (that is, any other matter relevant to the organization but not pertinent to the business then before the assembly), which can be addressed as the point is raised or deferred by the Chair to a later time in the meeting. An example of a procedural point would be a complaint by a member that the proceedings of the meeting cannot be heard because of excessive noise in the hall; an example of a non-procedural point would be a statement by a member publicly recognizing an honor received by another member that reflects favorably on the organization.

Postpone a motion   To delay the consideration of a motion to a later time in the same meeting or to another meeting.

Precedence   The priority with which matters pending before the assembly are considered.

Precedent   A ruling of the Chair or a decision by the assembly that sets a policy for that area of concern and that may indicate how an assembly should decide or act on similar matters in the future. A precedent is not binding, however.

Preference in recognition   The priority in which members are recognized by the Chair to speak; the order is determined by the purpose for which they seek recognition. For example, the maker of the main motion has preference in recognition over other members to speak on the main motion; however, a member who then seeks to raise a point of order has priority because the point of order has precedence over the main motion. *See* **Precedence.**

Preside   To conduct the business of a deliberative assembly.

Previous question   *See* **Close debate.**

Privileged motion   A motion of such urgency that it is heard immediately even though it interrupts pending business. An example of this type of motion is the motion to recess.

Procedural motion   *See* **Motion.**

Proposed agenda   *See* **Agenda.**

Proxy   A written authorization by an absent member for another member to cast that absent member's vote, either in a specific way on a particular matter or on matters in general. Proxies are not allowed in deliberative assemblies unless specifically authorized in the bylaws.

Put the question   The question by the Chair to the members of an assembly as to who favors and who opposes the pending motion, thus eliciting their decision by means of a vote.

Question   The issue or the proposal containing the motion before an assembly.

Quorum   The number or percentage of members required in the bylaws to be present at a meeting of an assembly in order for it to conduct business legally.

Recess   A brief adjournment or interruption of a meeting, which does not end the meeting.

Recognize   The selection by the Chair of the next member of the assembly to have the right to speak.

Reconsider   To consider again a vote previously taken.

Refer a motion   To send a motion to another body, such as a committee or the board of directors, for further consideration. This motion may include instructions to the body to which the motion is referred, such as to study the motion, to redraft it, and to report it back to the assembly at the next meeting.

Report   The communication by a committee or an officer to the assembly. A report can be written or verbal.

Request   Any petition by a member, through the Chair, to the assembly that does not require a suspension of the rules.

Rescind   To cancel or repeal a motion previously adopted.

Resolution   A statement of policy or position of an organization. Resolutions may also contain directions for action.

Roll call vote   A vote in which members respond for or against a proposal as each member's name is called.

Rules   A governance document of an organization, which contains provisions that direct how business will be conducted at its meetings following parliamentary procedure; sometimes referred to as rules of order. *See also* **Standing rules.**

Ruling   Any statement or act by the Chair that relates to or affects the procedure of the meeting.

Second   Support for a motion by a second member.

Seriatim   Consideration of a list of matters, item by item. *See also* **Division of the question; En bloc.**

Session   A series of successive meetings, usually over several days, all covered by the same notice and agenda.

Simple majority   Means the same as *majority,* which is more than half.

Special committee   A committee assigned a specific task for a limited time. Once the task is completed, the committee is terminated. *See also* **Committee.**

Special meeting   A meeting called for a time not provided for in the governance documents or the customary time for a meeting. No action can be taken at a special meeting except on those matters specified in the call for that meeting.

Staggered terms   Terms of board or committee members arranged in such a way that only a certain portion of the members' terms end in a given year. For example, nine members of a standing committee could have staggered three-year terms so that only three members' terms end each year and the other six continue, thus providing continuity for the committee.

Standing committee   A committee established in the governance documents that continues in existence, or "stands," from year to year, considering the subject matter assigned to it and making proposals on a regular basis. *See also* **Committee.**

Standing division   *See* **Division, in voting.**

Standing rules   The rules of an organization that continue from meeting to meeting.

State the question   Restatement of a motion by the Chair after it has been moved and seconded, thus ruling it in order and initiating its consideration through debate.

Substantive motion   A proposal to an assembly for a decision that does not relate to procedure.

Substitution   An amendment that both deletes and adds, thus proposing an alternative to the pending motion. Also referred to as a substitute motion, it may propose a substitute for the entire pending motion or a portion of the pending motion. *See also* **Amend.**

Suspend   To make ineffective for a limited period of time, as in the case of suspending a rule, which means that the rule suspended will be of no effect for the remainder of the meeting, or for the time designated in the motion to suspend.

Table   A motion to postpone that is not recommended in this book because it postpones and in practice often kills the pending motion without debate and vote by a simple majority.

Tally   To count the votes of the members in an assembly for and against a motion or to count the votes for the candidates in an election. The tally is a specific count, as opposed to the Chair's estimate on a voice vote or a standing division vote. *See also* **Vote.**

Teller's committee   The committee of the assembly which has the duty of performing the tally of the votes and then reporting the results back to the assembly.

Term of office   The period of time, set in the bylaws, that a member serves in office after appointment or election.

Tie vote   A vote in which the affirmative votes equal the negative votes. The motion or candidate, therefore, does not succeed for lack of a majority.

Two-thirds vote   At least two-thirds of the votes cast. Also called a two-thirds majority.

Unanimous consent   A vote by the assembly in which no opposition is voiced upon a call by the Chair for any objection.

Unfinished business   A matter postponed from a previous meeting.

Voice vote   A vote in which members say aye or no in unison and the Chair estimates the result according to the loudness of each.

Vote   The method used in a deliberative assembly by which the members indicate their wish to accept or reject a candidate or proposal. *For methods of voting, see* **Ballot; Counted vote; Division, in voting; Roll call vote; Voice vote.** *For types of vote results, see* **Acclamation; Illegal vote; Majority vote; Plurality vote; Simple majority; Tie vote; Two-thirds vote; Unanimous consent.**

Vote immediately   See **Close Debate.**

Index

THE TWELVE BASIC MOTIONS

Basic Motion	Debatable	Vote Required	Amendable	See page:
Main Motion	Yes	Majority	Yes	97–103
Amend	Yes	Majority	Yes	103
Postpone (to a certain time)	Yes	Majority	Yes	105
Refer	Yes	Majority	Yes	105
Close Debate	No	2/3	No	109
Divide the Question	Yes	Majority	Yes	112
Motions Relating to Voting	No	Majority (except for divisions and roll call votes)	No	112
Reconsider	Yes	See comments	No	126
Request (to the assembly to allow something)	No	Majority	No	111
Suspend the Rules	No	2/3	No	75
Appeal	Yes	Majority	No	115
Adjourn	No	Majority	No, but see comments	136